IMAGES OF WAR

M2/M3 BRADLEY

RARE PHOTOGRAPHS FROM WARTIME ARCHIVES

DAVID DOYLE

Pen & Sword
MILITARY
AN IMPRINT OF PEN & SWORD BOOKS LTD.
YORKSHIRE – PHILADELPHIA

First published in Great Britain in 2018 by
Pen & Sword Military
An imprint of
Pen & Sword Books Ltd
Yorkshire – Philadelphia

ISBN 978 1 52673 881 3

A CIP catalogue record for this book is available from the British Library.

Typeset in 12/14.5 Gill Sans by
Aura Technology and Software Services, India
Printed and bound in Europe by Printworks Global Ltd

Pen & Sword Books Limited incorporates the imprints of Atlas, Archaeology, Aviation, Discovery, Family History, Fiction, History, Maritime, Military, Military Classics, Politics, Select, Transport, True Crime, Air World, Frontline Publishing, Leo Cooper, Remember When, Seaforth Publishing, The Praetorian Press, Wharncliffe Local History, Wharncliffe Transport, Wharncliffe True Crime and White Owl.

For a complete list of Pen & Sword titles please contact

PEN & SWORD BOOKS LIMITED
47 Church Street, Barnsley, South Yorkshire, S70 2AS, England
E-mail: enquiries@pen-and-sword.co.uk
Website: www.pen-and-sword.co.uk

or
PEN AND SWORD BOOKS
1950 Lawrence Rd, Havertown, PA 19083, USA
E-mail: Uspen-and-sword@casematepublishers.com
Website: www.penandswordbooks.com

IMAGES OF WAR

M2/M3 BRADLEY

Cover: A US Army Bradley fighting vehicle assigned to the 3rd Infantry Division is engaged in a situation-training exercise at Fort Stewart, Georgia, on 27 February 2007. The large stowage rack on the side of the vehicle was not a typical feature. (DoD)

Title: A US Army M2A3 Bradley infantry fighting vehicle (IFV) advances towards a footbridge used as an escape route by terrorist and insurgent forces during Operation Orange Justice in Buhriz, Iraq, on 11 February 2007. The vehicle features explosive reactive armor (ERA) tiles on the side and the front of the hull and the turret, and a ballistic shield for the commander on top of the turret. (DoD)

Contents

Acknowledgments

This book would not have been possible without the generous help of Rob Ervin, Tom Kailbourn, Don Moriarty, Gary Owsley, Chris Hughes, Lt. Col. (retired) John Charvat, Paul Bird, Scott Taylor and the staffs of the Ordnance and Patton Museums, as well as the Public Affairs team at the Third Armored Cavalry Regiment. Special thanks go to my wife Denise, who accompanied me through hot and cold as these vehicles were photographed, and never failed to provide a word of encouragement when needed.

Introduction

The US Army had purchased the M113 beginning in 1960 to use as its main armored personnel carrier. It proved to be an extremely versatile vehicle, but in its APC role it was found wanting. A vehicle was needed that had some offensive firepower, provided protection from the threats of a nuclear, chemical, or biological battlefield, and kept pace with the next anticipated generation of tanks. Various attempts were made, beginning in the late 1960s, but not until the mid-1970s did a vehicle begin to take shape that would eventually lead to the new infantry fighting vehicle.

The M113 served the US Army for decades after its development in the late 1950s. It was designed to provide troops some degree of protection while carrying them to combat, and then troops had to dismount to fight.

FMC, the manufacturer of the M113, developed two vehicles, the XM765 and XM723, that shared suspension components with the amphibious LVTP family of vehicles. With some modifications the XM723 became what is known today as the M2/M3 Bradley family, named after the Second World War US General Omar Bradley. The new vehicle entered service with US troops in 1981. It was built around the formidable Bushmaster 25mm chain gun in a two-man turret. The three-man crew was augmented by the ability to carry an infantry team of seven soldiers in the rear compartment protected by the aluminum alloy armored skin. Its Cummins Diesel water-cooled V-8 engine gave it tremendous automotive performance. Thus began a thirty-year program of modification, modernization, and development that brought about the formidable weapons of today. FMC is part of the United Defense partnership that was purchased by BAE Systems in 2005, a British armaments manufacturer. They continue to produce and update older vehicles in the Bradley family.

The vehicle is also the basis of the M3 series, also known as Bradley, a scout vehicle for the cavalry. The M3 has the same three-man vehicle crew of driver, gunner and

Reacting to the introduction of the new Soviet BMP-1 with heavier armament and firing ports for the infantry, FMC developed the XM723. With a 20mm gun in the turret this served as a prototype for the Bradley series which replaced the M113.

commander, but only two scouts are carried in the rear compartment. Tactics have been adapted over the years to fit the vehicle's strengths.

The M2 Bradley was approved for production in January of 1980 and began to reach units in 1981. The first of the M2 infantry fighting vehicles and M3 cavalry fighting vehicles were equipped with a launcher for the then-standard TOW wire-guided anti-tank missile. The early vehicles are recognizable by the rounded laminate steel armor plates and skirts that cover the lower sides of the hull and suspension, and the fittings for firing ports on both hull sides. A total of 2,300 M2s and M3s were eventually produced.

Omar Nelson Bradley, one of only nine men to rise to the five-star rank of General of the Army, is the namesake of the M2/M3 family of vehicles. Bradley, who had the reputation of being the "FI's general," served on active duty continuously from August 1, 1911 until his death on April 8, 1981 - a total of 69 years, 8 months and 7 days. In addition to numerous commands during WWIII, after the war he also served as two-year stint as head of the Veteran's Administration, Army Chief of Staff and Chairman of the Joint Chiefs of Staff. This is the longest active duty career in the history of the United States Armed Forces.

Chapter 1

THE M2 AND XM2

The initial production version of the Bradley infantry fighting vehicle is the M2, later called M2A0 to avoid confusion from later variants. The only external difference from the M2A1 is the shorter TOW missile launcher. They began to reach infantry units in 1981, giving them unprecedented firepower, speed, and protection. The TOW missiles gave the vehicle the ability to destroy any armored vehicle that it faced on the battlefield.

Above: Very little preparation was necessary to make the Bradley amphibious. The trim vane was folded forward and the water barrier erected by installing supports down the hull side. The tracks propelled the vehicle in the water.

Opposite above: The trim vane created a tall bow at the front of the vehicle which allowed it to take a nose-up attitude in the water. This was necessary to create sufficient freeboard along the side water barrier.

Opposite below: The trim vane could also be folded forward to create a flat work platform for servicing the engine. The angled covers over the headlights made contact with the hull to seal this area for flotation when the vane was raised.

NASTY
BOYZ

NON ARMOR
NASTY BOYZ

Above: The Bradley mounts a small two-man turret with the commander on the right side of the main gun and the gunner on the left. Both crewmen are provided a hatch, the commander's being more dome-shaped for use of the periscopes.

Opposite above: The upper portion of the glacis armor to the right of the driver covers the engine compartment. The M2 and M2A1 were powered by the VTA-903T a Diesel engine manufactured by Cummins which produced 450 hp.

Opposite below: The air intake screen in the center of the forward section of the upper hull feeds air to the radiator below, which is mounted directly above the engine. The coaxial machine gun is missing from its armored shroud in the turret.

Above: The turret shell was made from aluminum alloy armor with its front section covered with a thin layer of steel armor laminate. This gave it protection against Soviet 14.5mm machine guns and 152mm artillery splinters.

Below: This vehicle is missing the rear turret stowage bin giving a good view of the construction of the various rolled aluminum plate panels. The plates are angled to provide greater protection against penetration.

Above: The turret's left side does not have the same sloped armor as the right but has the added protection of the armored box encasing the TOW missile launcher. A lift ring is on the left rear of the turret.

Below: The commander's hatch hinge has three notches for opening to different positions: raised to provide overhead protection, open to vertical to provide back protection, and fully opened.

The M2 is equipped with the initial twin TOW missile launcher which fired the original shorter 48.5 inch missile. The launcher was updated to fire the TOW 2 on the M2A1 model.

The launcher is basically an armored box loaded from the rear which holds the disposable launch tubes for the TOW missiles. The launcher is loaded by a crew man through the rear compartment roof hatch.

Above: On the left side turret roof is the armored cover for the gunner's Integrated Sight Unit (ISU). This is the primary sight for the main gun and the co-ax machine gun. It is equipped with a relay sight for the commander.

Below: The left side of the M2 Bradley IFV hull is covered with a section of curved laminate armor plate. The bottom of this armor extends down to protect the lower hull and suspension. This lower section is hinged to allow access to suspension components for maintenance and repair. The paint on the rubber portion of the rim makes their dimensions a bit deceiving.

Above: The left rear side of the hull has brackets and a rack for storing elements of the flotation water barrier. This equipment was eliminated on the M2A2 Bradley.

Opposite above: The driver's hatch has a domed shape allowing the driver's seat to remain in one position with the hatch open or closed. The hatch is equipped with four fixed periscopes; a passive night sight can be used for night driving.

Opposite below: There is a periscope mounted in the left side hull roof for one of the infantry passengers seated just behind the driver, ahead of the turret basket. The firing port weapon can be sighted from this periscope.

Above: The rear section of the side armored skirt is hinged to allow access to the suspension and idler wheel. The idler wheel at the rear is used to properly adjust track tension. At the lower edge of the skirt is a crew step.

Opposite above: Looking back towards the rear of the vehicle from beneath the turret overhang is located the rear periscope for aiming the left side firing port weapon. The turret ring area is protected by an armored skirt at the base of the turret.

Opposite below: The pole-like devices at the left rear are upright supports for the water barrier side curtain. The Bradley was only able to cross calm inland waterways. Many drownings occurred during amphibious operation of the early variants.

Above: The roof of the rear compartment is equipped with a large cargo hatch which is hinged to open to the rear. The turret is traversed slightly left to allow a crewman to reload the TOW missile launcher with some protection of the hatch lid.

Below: The missing turret bustle stowage bin affords an excellent view of the hull roof, forward of the cargo hatch.

To the rear of the hatch are three fixed periscopes mounted in the hull roof. The periscopes give the infantry squad some vision outside the vehicle and can be used for sighting firing-port weapons in the ramp ports.

The M2's rear infantry ramp is equipped with a door in its left side and two firing ports. It is hinged at the bottom. The door allows access to the interior without lowering the powered ramp. The ramp's two firing ports allow the crew to fire fully-automatic 5.56mm firing-point weapons from within the protection of the vehicle's armor.

Above: Brackets for stowing a tow cable are mounted to the right side of the ramp. The firing port openings have been blanked off on this example. The tow pintle is attached just below the lower edge of the ramp.

Below: Both rear corners of the hull outboard of the ramp are fitted with stowage lockers. These provide some additional ammunition storage and storage for mines outside the protective armor of the vehicle.

Above: The initial production M2 Bradley was 21 feet 2 inches long, 9 feet 9 inches tall over the commander's hatch, and 10 feet 6 inches wide. Combat loaded it weighed just over 25 tons. It carried a crew of 9 men. With a 450 horsepower engine the vehicle was capable of keeping pace with the new gas turbine-powered M1 Abrams tank.

Opposite above: Unlike the M113 that it replaced, the Bradley was designed to allow its crew to fight from the vehicle's interior from firing ports on the hull sides and rear doors. The hull side ports were eliminated on the M2A1 variant. The Bradley truly lived up to the name infantry fighting vehicle.

Opposite below: The right rear firing ports are covered by additional steel armor. Special firing port weapons, known as the M231, similar to the M16, were provided for the infantry passengers. The weapons fired only at full automatic and had no safety.

Above: The Bradley is equipped with 6 pairs of 24x4 inch road wheels per side. The first, second and last road wheel stations are equipped with shock absorbers. The idler wheel is a steel casting with a center hub carrying a lubrication point.

Opposite above: The roof cargo hatch is seen here from the right side. The cast lift ring is bolted to the hull armor rather than welded. This decreases the risk of fracturing the aluminum armor under the weight of the lifted vehicle.

Opposite below: M3 CFVs can be identified by the cargo hatch cover mounting periscopes rather than the rear of the hull roof. On this M2 Bradley the right side periscope openings have been blanked off with sheet metal.

This XM2 is preserved on the ground of Fort Benning, Georgia. Following testing of the XM2 prototypes, delivery of serial production M2 IFV began in May 1981, and the vehicle was officially named in honor of General Omar Bradley during a 20 October 1981 ceremony at Ft. Myer, Va.

Above: This vehicle is fitted with the rear turret bustle storage bin that was used for storing additional 25mm ammunition. The rear of the rack was made from armor plate and angled to increase protection of the turret rear.

Below: This preserved XM2 is equipped with the smoke grenade launchers on the front of each side of the turret. The boxes above the launchers are for stowage of additional smoke grenade ammunition.

Chapter 2

The M2A2 ODS (Operation Desert Storm)

Above: The M2A2 with its new armor protection began to reach units in 1988 and was very common on the battlefield of the first Gulf War of 1991. The added weight of the armor brought the end of the Bradley's amphibious capability. This example is the later M2A2 ODS which includes a number of features added to the vehicles following Operation Desert Storm. These included a thermal vision device for the driver, a combat identification system, a global positioning system, an eye-safe laser rangefinder, and a missile countermeasure system. (Gary Owsley)

Opposite above: The trim vane associated with the earlier water barrier was eliminated from the M2A2. Large plates of laminated spaced steel armor were added to the glacis. New headlight mounts and guards were also installed. (Gary Owsley)

Opposite below: The new appliqué armor covered the entire front of the vehicle. The lower hull front plate armor fits around the contours of the final drive housings. The bolts on the plates are for the addition of reactive armor boxes. (Gary Owsley)

Above: Army regulations state that the vehicle should not be operated outside a motor pool with the driver's hatch in the open position. Lacking any air conditioning, Bradleys are seen in Iraq driving with them open. (Gary Owsley)

Opposite above: The driver's hatch is equipped with 4 fixed periscopes; the center periscope can be replaced with a passive night vision device for night time driving. The appliqué armor plates are coated with a non-skid texture. (Gary Owsley)

Opposite below: The handle on the interior of the hatch is for changing its position. The assist springs within the hinge mechanism making opening and closing the heavy hatch quite simple. The posts beside the driver's station are wire cutters. (Gary Owsley)

THIS SIDE OFF

THIS SIDE OFF

Above: The drive sprockets are mounted at the front of the vehicle. With the increased weight of the new armor package the power train was improved to maintain performance levels. The Cummins Diesel now produced 600 horsepower. (Gary Owsley)

Opposite above: All of the vision devices on the M2A2 are laser shielded. This protects the crews vision from damage from lasers used for various purposes on the battlefield. The periscopes lenses appear different colors depending on viewing angle. (Gary Owsley)

Opposite below: The new laminate armor plates on the M2A2 are made up of two ¼-inch armor plates spaced 1 inch apart. They are hinged on the lower skirt portion to allow access to the vehicles suspension for maintenance. (Gary Owsley)

IN CASE
OF FIRE
PULL HANDLE
THIS SIDE OFF

Above: The laminate armor plate array protects the entire length of the Bradley's hull side. The lower skirts are spaced away from the top plate to clear the tracks. The spaced arrangement of the armor plate is apparent on the lowered ramp. (Gary Owsley)

Opposite above: A number of Bradley IFVs were destroyed in the first Gulf War by friendly fire incidents. Thermal recognition panels were developed to give Allied vehicles an easily recognizable appearance through thermal imaging sights. (Gary Owsley)

Opposite below: The left side of the turret mounts the twin launcher for the TOW 2 missiles. The launcher is also capable of firing the Improved TOW with its secondary warhead for defeating explosive reactive armor. (Gary Owsley)

Above: The additional armor plate added to the M2A2 is fitted to the rear ramp with a space to allow for some stand-off protection. The plate is cut and contoured to fit around the tow lugs and towing pintle. (Gary Owsley)

Opposite above: The paired road wheels on the Bradley family vehicles are aluminum castings bolted to a central hub that carries a lubricated wheel bearing. The solid rubber tire is pressed onto and bonded to the wheel casting. (Gary Owsley)

Opposite below: The rear ramp is lowered on this M2A2 ODS. The ramp's position is controlled electronically and powered hydraulically and takes approximately 5 seconds to lower. The interior lights of the rear compartment automatically turn off when the ramp is opened. The identification panels are specially contoured to fit the rear hull corner stowage boxes. The infantry complement of the M2A2 was reduced to six making for a total crew of nine. (Gary Owsley)

The appliqué plate for the door within the ramp is spaced further out and is larger than the hole in the ramp plate; this covers the gap between the door section and the ramp section. (Gary Owsley)

The bottom of the ramp is fitted with a standard US-style towing pintle. The pintle has a locking clamp that allows a trailer to be pulled without a safety chain. (Gary Owsley)

The inside surface of the ramp is kept as free from impediments as possible to allow a quick exit for the infantry. The circular hinged plates in the ramp are access covers for the firing ports. (Gary Owsley)

The right side of the ramp retains the cable stowage fittings. All the closures on the cable stowage and stowage boxes are quick release rubber latches. (Gary Owsley)

The stowage bins on the rear corners of the hull were designed not only to free up interior space for the occupants, but also to store dangerous items such as additional ammunition and mines away from the crew. (Gary Owsley)

The interior surface of the ramp has the textured anti-skid coating to improve footing when the ramp is wet. The attachment arm for the hydraulic actuator is at the lower left of the ramp. (Gary Owsley)

The right side of the compartment behind the protective wall for the turret ring is fitted with 4 folding crew seats. The right side sponson area serves for storage of ammunition, and a Dragon anti-tank missile launcher. (Gary Owsley)

More dangerous cargo is stored in the right hand rear stowage box. Positions are clearly marked for items such as grenades, flares, anti-personnel mines, and a Claymore mine. The door has a rubber seal. (Gary Owsley)

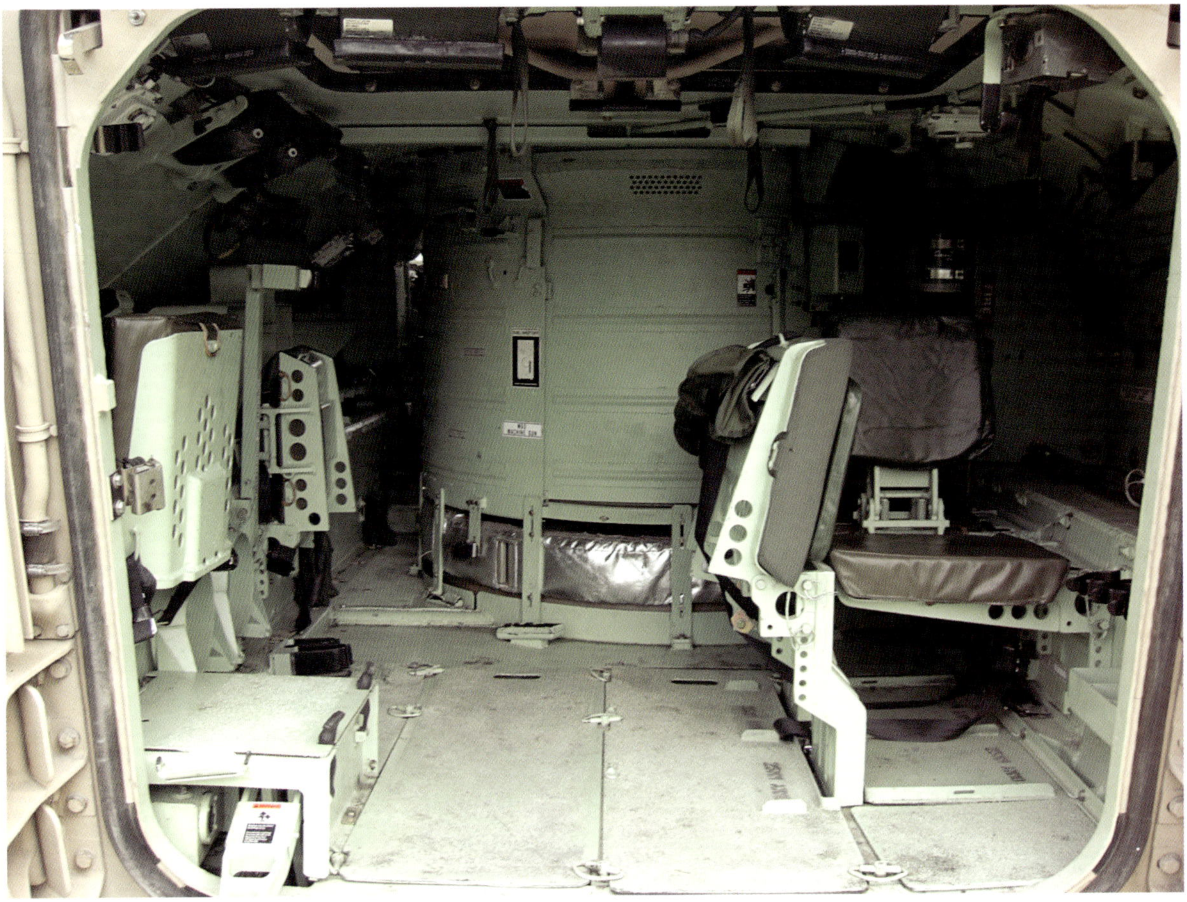

The left side of the compartment has two additional folding seats. The crew seat directly behind the driver was eliminated from the M2A2. The doors in the floor provide access to additional ammunition stowage. (Gary Owsley)

One of the infantry seats is folded into the seating position. They can be folded up to the right to clear more floor space. The clips on the wall to the rear of the seat are from storing LAW anti-tank weapons. (Gary Owsley)

The folding seats are fitted with canvas bins for personal items on their bottom sides. The protective wall for the turret basket is seen here with its sliding door open. This allows turret crew access to the rear of the hull. (Gary Owsley)

The open door provides a view into the lower portion of the turret basket. The black panel at the top center is the gunner's main control for the turret weapons. The 2 handles adjust the seat heights. (Gary Owsley)

NIGHT SIGHT DOOR HANDLE
Turn off power before connecting or disconnecting electrical plugs. Failure to do so could damage equipment.
CAUTION
HEARING PROTECTION REQUIRED
Wear both headphones and earplugs
TRIGGER
GRENADE LAUNCHER

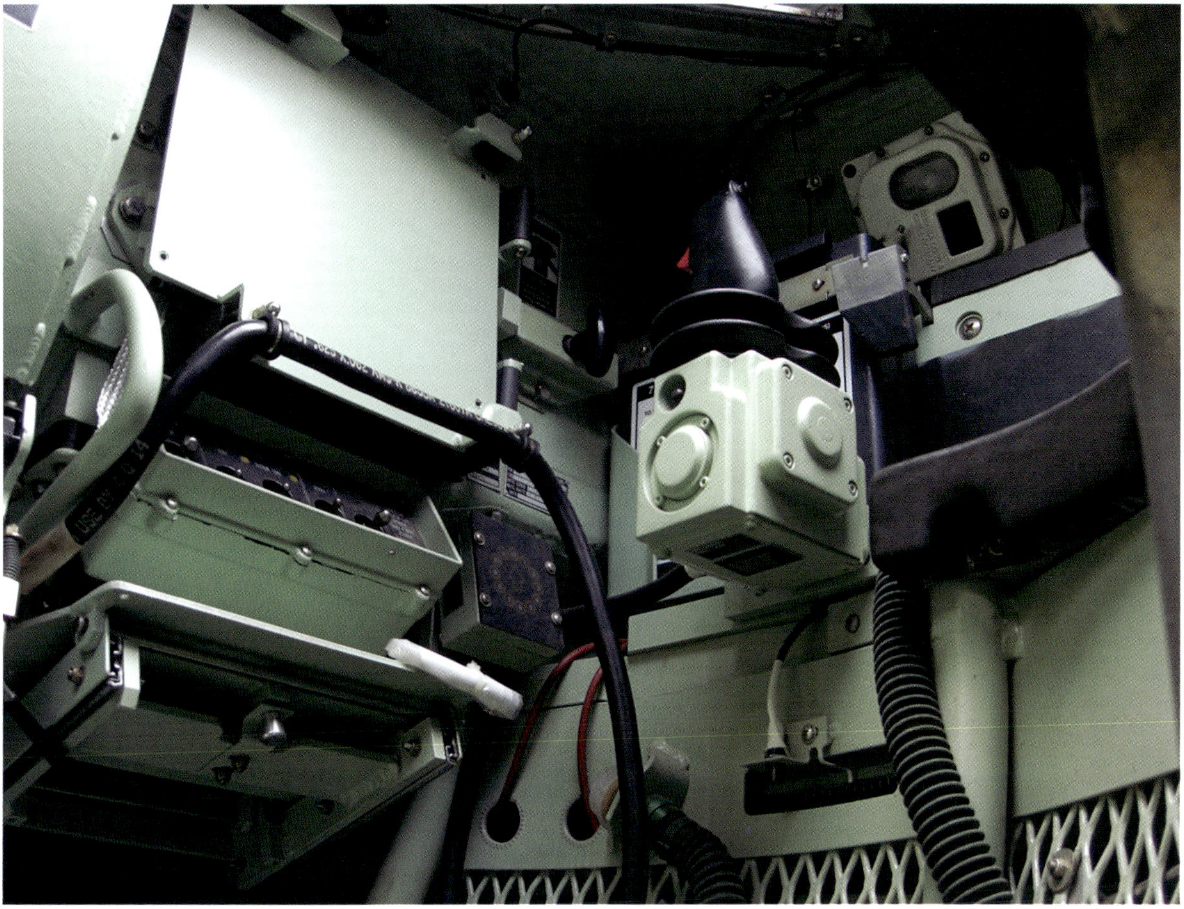

Above: To the left side is the commander's hand control to traverse the turret. At any time the commander can override the gunner's controls except when a TOW missile is in flight to its target. (Gary Owsley)

Opposite above: The gunner controls his selection of ammunition type and the particular weapon from this control panel. He can also fire the smoke grenades from this position. The panel is easily reached by the gunner or commander. (Gary Owsley)

Opposite below: The traverse of the turret and elevation of the main weapons are controlled by the dual hand control that houses the triggers as well. The gunner's ISU is just above the hand controls. (Gary Owsley)

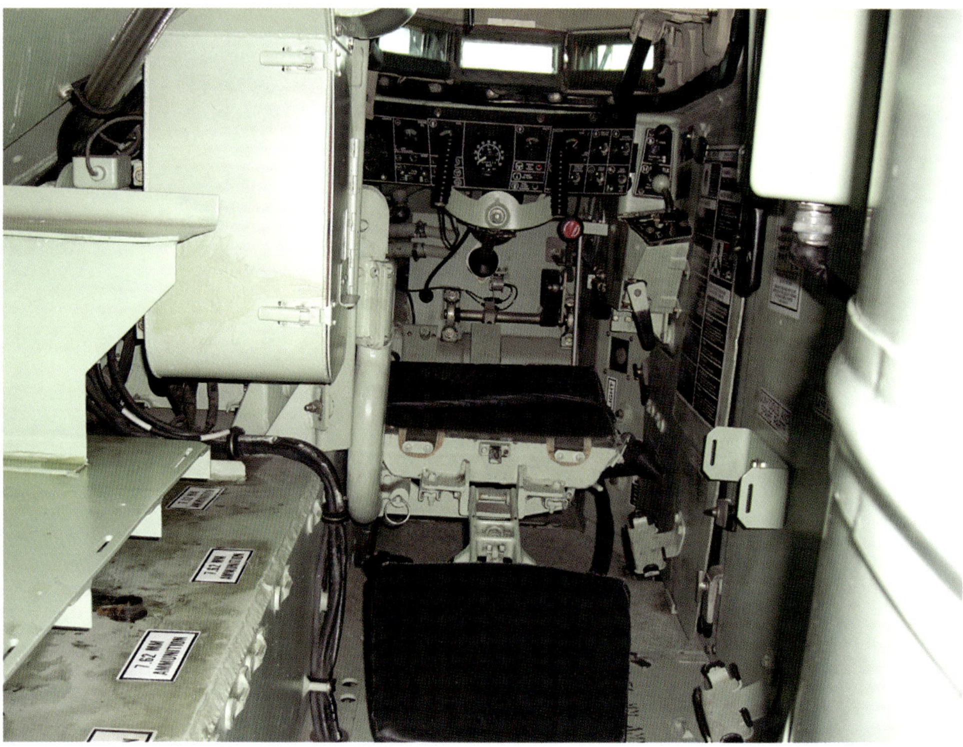
7.62 MM AMMUNITION

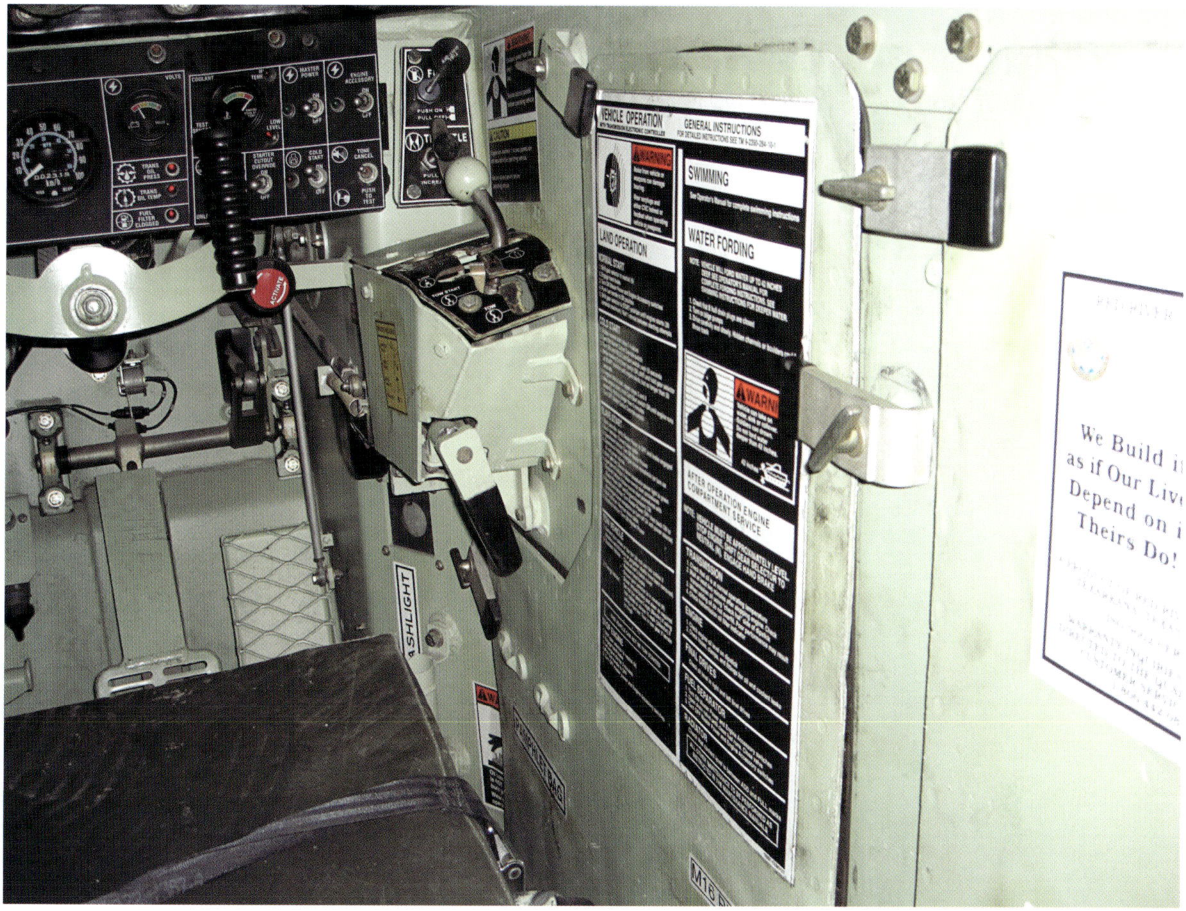

Above: On the left wall of the driver's compartment is the transmission selector handle. The driver selects a setting, and the vehicle matches engine speed to a proper gear for most efficient operation from accelerator pedal input. (Gary Owsley)

Opposite above: A view into the left rear compartment where racks for stowage of two Dragon anti-tank missile launchers and the infantry squad's weapons are found between the folding seats. Web handles are attached to the roof for the crew. (Gary Owsley)

Opposite below: The driver's position is in the left front of the vehicle alongside the engine and transmission. This seat back folds down allowing access to the area from the rear compartment. The steering wheel is at the center. (Gary Owsley)

Above: The driver's controls are very similar to a normal automobile with an automatic transmission; gear selector, steering yoke, accelerator and brake. The three-switch fixture to the left is the main electrical control. (Gary Owsley)

Opposite above: With the addition of the armor package on the M2A2 the weight of the vehicle was up to approximately 30 tons, and 33 with the reactive armor tiles added. This weight is equal to a WWII M4 Sherman tank. (Gary Owsley)

Opposite below: The rear ramp is seen here open from the right side. The appliqué armor kit included a steel armor panel for the belly of the hull for additional protection from land mines. (Gary Owsley)

MV03FU

The M231 Firing Port Weapon was similar to an M16 but lacked a butt stock. Its barrel had a threaded fitting to lock into the firing port. It fired only on fully automatic and lacked a safety. The M2A2 was issued with 2. (Gary Owsley)

The addition of the armor plates meant the elimination of the firing ports from the sides of the vehicle. Many commanders saw them as having little benefit and the port weapons as a safety issue to the crew. (Gary Owsley)

Above: The periscopes were retained in the sides of the rear compartment to give the infantry passengers some view of the battlefield. The external control for the interior fire suppression system is at the right rear of the hull. (Gary Owsley)

Below: The additional armor kits added to the M2A2 and M3A2 CFV gave added protection from penetration by shaped charge anti-tank missiles. A spall liner was added to the interior for added protection for the crew. (Gary Owsley)

Above: The armor kits also covered the multiple facets of the turret. The many fasteners on the surfaces of the plates allow an additional reactive armor kit to be bolted to the exterior. (Gary Owsley)

Below: The M2A2 also received a revised exit and armored box for the engine exhaust. The box has internal insulation to protect the crew from the heat of the exhaust. (Gary Owsley)

The top of the exhaust box is hinged for access to the pipe within. The hinged plates on the forward faces of the turret are part of the thermal combat recognition system new to the M2A2 ODS. (Gary Owsley)

The addition of the armored plates and elimination of the trim vane brought about the need for a new headlight suite on the M2A2. The heavy steel guard for the right side headlight is seen here from the rear. (Gary Owsley)

2350-01-248-7619

Above: The lower hull front plate has cast armored bulges that house the final drives. This is a gear reduction system that transfers power from the transmission output shafts to the drive sprockets. (Gary Owsley)

Opposite above: The thickness of the headlight guard is evident from the front. It provides not only protection against damage from striking objects but also from small arms fire from the rear and sides. (Gary Owsley)

Opposite below: The laminate armor plates are cut to fit around the lower front hull tow lugs and final drive humps on the lower front plate. The thickness of the plate laminations is an inch and a half. (Gary Owsley)

Above: The right side hull lift ring is moved to a position bolted to the appliqué armor plate. This view gives good detail of all of the plate edges, fasteners, and the non-skid coating added to the plates. (Gary Owsley)

Opposite above: The final drive housings are large armored castings welded to the lower hull aluminum plates. The inner plate is bolted on to allow access to the inner spur gear of the final drive. Additional access requires removal of the drive sprocket. (Gary Owsley)

Opposite below: The front fenders of the M2A2 are made of rubber to avoid damage from striking objects or from debris picked up by the track. The flexible rubber does not retain paint well and is flaking on this example. (Gary Owsley)

The driver's compartment is relatively spacious and the seating position comfortable. The area is notoriously hot in service in Iraq, being separated from the Diesel engine by only a thin wall with some insulation. (Gary Owsley)

The air intake and protective screen are centered above the engine to the right of the driver's hatch. The Cummins VTA-903T engine's output was increased to 600 horse power for the M2A2 and M3A3 Bradleys. (Gary Owsley)

The air intake is just below the centerline of the turret, which is offset to the right of the vehicle. This allows more room for the rear compartment passengers. The stowage boxes are for smoke grenade rounds. (Gary Owsley)

The barrel of the M242 25mm Bushmaster chain gun is equipped with a muzzle brake. The brake deflects some of the gases as the projectile exits the barrel to the rear, thus reducing recoil by about 10 percent. (Gary Owsley)

THIS SIDE OFF

Above: The M240 is manufactured by FN of Belgium and is capable of firing ball, AP, and tracer ammunition to an effective range of about two miles. Tracer burnout is at approximately 1000 yards. (Gary Owsley)

Opposite above: The 25mm Bushmaster's barrel is over 6 ½ feet long. The flutes in the barrel give it added strength without excessively increasing weight. Many barrels have been bent on Bradleys in the urban fighting in Iraq. (Gary Owsley)

Opposite below: The appliqué armor kits added to the M2A2 turret brought about the removal of the armored shroud for the coaxial mounted M240 7.62mm machine gun. The storage of smoke grenades was also relocated. (Gary Owsley)

The turret front is fitted with folding panels that are a part of the M2A2's combat identification system. These provide a distinctive view for gunners when seen through thermal sights on Allied vehicles. (Gary Owsley)

The Bradley IFV and CFV are equipped with the M257 Smoke Grenade Launcher on each side of the front of the turret. The cast aluminum launcher fires 4 muzzle-loaded 66mm grenades to approximately 30 yards. (Gary Owsley)

Above: The right side arrangement of the appliqué armor package on the M2A2 is quite complex. It is contoured around the facets of the turret and has a cut out in the upper plate for the turret side antenna mount.

Below: The stowage on the left rear corner of the hull was revised with no need for the equipment for the water barrier. A total of 3,053 M2A2 and M3A2s were produced and many more were converted from earlier variants. (Gary Owsley)

Above: The turret bustle stowage bins is equipped with additional containers for stowing 25mm ammunition. The turret on the Bradley can traverse 360 degrees in approximately 6 seconds. (Gary Owsley)

Opposite above: The M2A2 and M2A3 retained the twin launcher for the TOW 2. The launcher had an elevation range between +29 and -19 degrees, but could only be fired from a slope of less than 10 degrees. (Gary Owsley)

Opposite below: The rear section of the twin TOW 2 launcher is hinged to allow access to the interior. The M2 Bradley series carried 5 TOW missiles internally; the M3 series had provisions to carry 10 missiles. (Gary Owsley)

Above: The hinge mechanism of the launcher is exposed when raised to the firing position. The launcher takes 5 to 6 seconds to raise; the missile can take 22 seconds to reach its maximum range of more than 2 miles. (Gary Owsley)

Opposite above: The opening on the front of the launcher is protected by an armored cover that stays in position even when the launcher is raised to the firing position, exposing the TOW tubes. (Gary Owsley)

Opposite below: With the launcher elevated to the firing position the appliqué armor plates of the left turret side are visible. An armored skirt surrounds the turret ring to deflect incoming shots in this area. (Gary Owsley)

Above: The TOW missile follows the gunner's line of sight to the target and is controlled through a wire that trails the unit in flight. The gunner merely keeps the crosshairs of his sight on the target. (Gary Owsley)

Opposite above: The electrical wiring to the firing connections is protected from chafing during operation by a rubber sleeve. The internal tubes of the launcher are visible through the opening in the underside. (Gary Owsley)

Opposite below: The elevation mechanism is protected by a cast armored housing. The appliqué armor kit extends forward on the left side behind the TOW launcher. (Gary Owsley)

IS SIDE OFF

Above: The Integrated Sighting Unit provides day or night vision with an infrared system. The gunner can choose between 4X and 12 X magnification of a target through his sight. (Gary Owsley)

Opposite above: The front armored cover for the launcher has a turn buckle type fitting to adjust the cover in relationship to the opening on the launcher. The cutout in the left turret plate fits over the lift ring. (Gary Owsley)

Opposite below: The M2A2 ODS also received modifications to the gunner's sighting system. An eye-safe laser rangefinder was added to the ISU which helped the gunner achieve high first shot hit probability without ranging fire.

The ISU is protected by an armored box on the left side turret roof with armored shutters. The mechanical link to the main gun was added with the laser rangefinder in the A2 model. (Gary Owsley)

The gunner's open hatch is at the bottom in this view of the rear of the housing for the Integrated Sight Unit (ISU). The three fanned-out tubes on the upper left of the ISU are holders for small flags. On top of the ISU is a holder for an anti-antitank-missile countermeasure device that was planned for the Bradley but did not become operational. (Gary Owsley)

The interior of the ISU is fitted with a single eye piece for the gunner and a relay sight for the commander. Below and to the right of the eye piece is the TOW launcher control. To the left are sight-setting controls. (Gary Owsley)

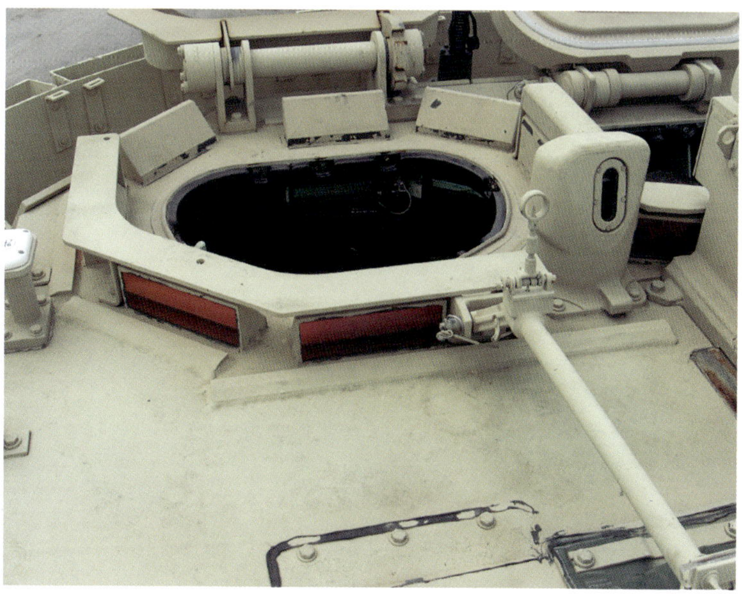

The M2A2 Bradley retains the mechanical link to the main gun for the commander's external recticle sight. To the right side of the hatch is an antenna for the GPS system added with the ODS upgrade. (Gary Owsley)

CAUTION
Turn off power before connecting or disconnecting electrical plugs. Failure to do so could damage equipment.

Above: The commander is provided with 6 fixed M17 laser protected periscopes around his hatch. The hatch lid is dome-shaped to allow better access to these periscopes. (Gary Owsley)

Opposite above: The commander's station has an eye piece for the relay sight tied to the gunner's ISU. This allows the commander to see the same sight picture as the gunner. The hatch opening is lined with rubber pads. (Gary Owsley)

Opposite below: The proximity of the hatch openings gives a good idea of how tight the confines of the turret are and just how closely the commander and gunner work in combat. (Gary Owsley)

The turret's right side is fitted with a GPS antenna and an antenna with a cage-like guard. The M2A2 is equipped with the AN/VRC-46 and AN/GRC-160 radio systems. (Gary Owsley)

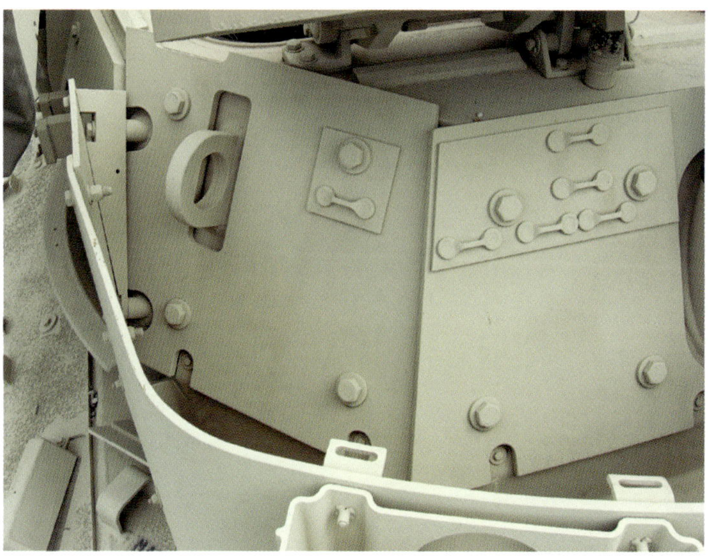

The appliqué armor kit for the turret covers the left rear corners with cut outs for the bustle rack mount and the rear lift ring. Tie-down points are provided on the turret rear and bustle edge for securing stowage. (Gary Owsley)

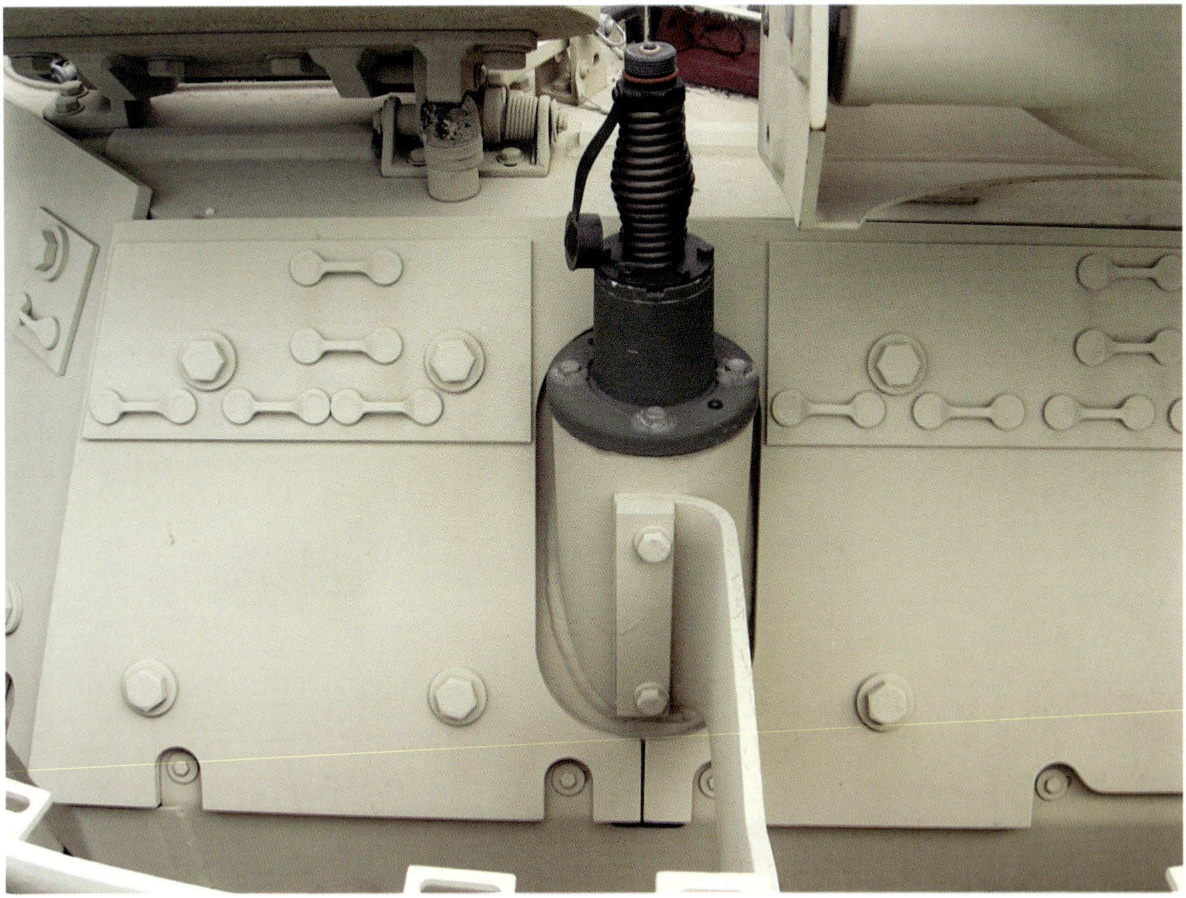

The center mount for the turret bustle stowage rack attaches to the rear antenna mount. The gunner's hatch is open and contacts the rubber bumper at the top left of the photo. (Gary Owsley)

Both the bustle rack and the smaller ammunition storage bins have perforations in their floors for drainage. The bustle rack is made from armored plate and provides stand-off protection for the turret rear. (Gary Owsley)

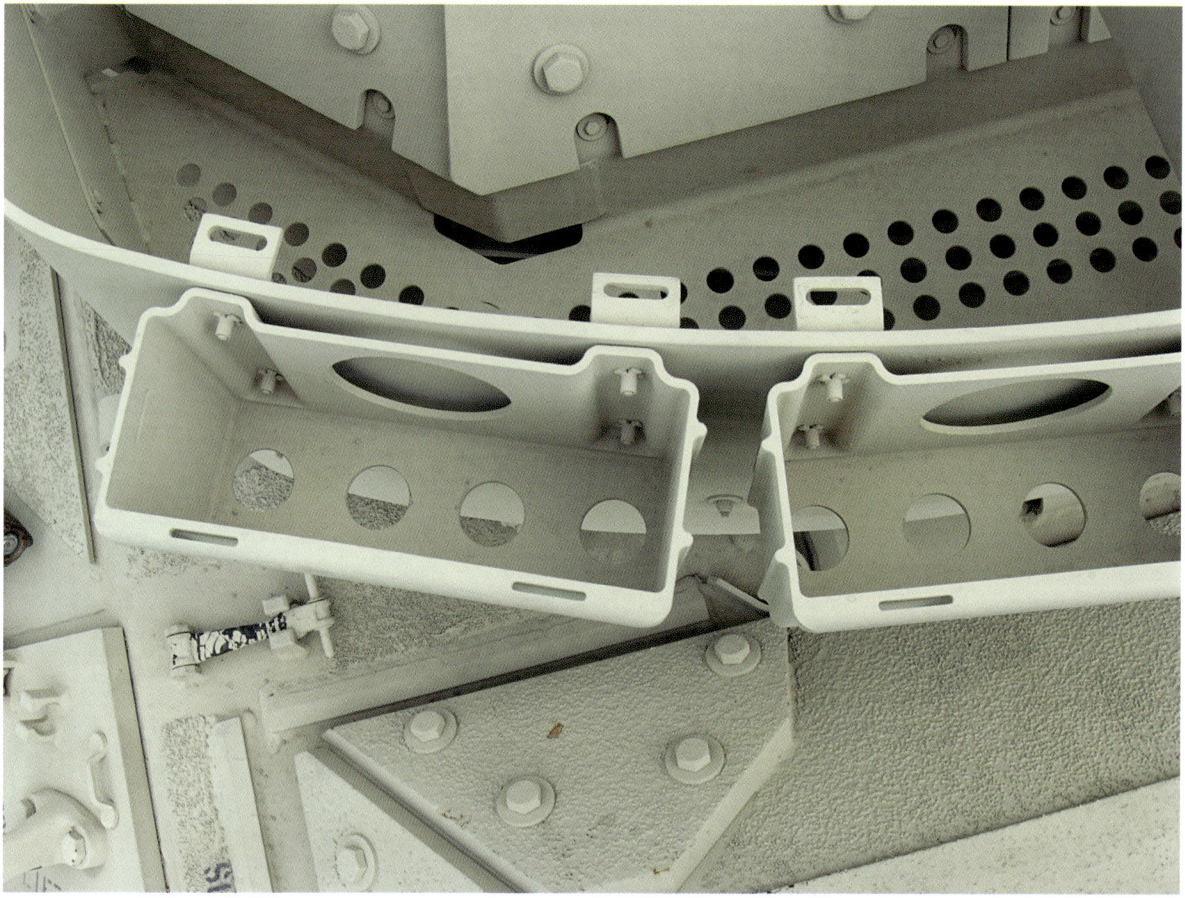

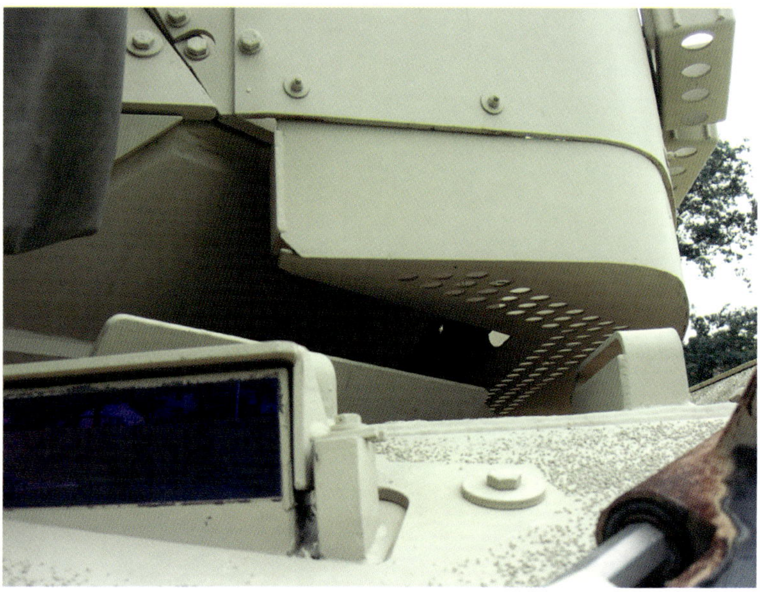

There are 5 of the small bins for 25mm ammunition attached to the bustle rack. The appliqué armor kit also provides plates for the sides and edges of the front of the hull roof cargo hatch. (Gary Owsley)

The turret bustle rack, seen here from below, provides additional external stowage for the crew's personal items. Bradley IFVs are often seen in Iraq with their sides and turrets covered in the crew's belongings. (Gary Owsley)

The roof hatch also is equipped with an appliqué plate on its top. The protective guards of the roof periscopes are seen to the rear of the hatch. Storage brackets for various tools and fittings are on the left rear of the hull. (Gary Owsley)

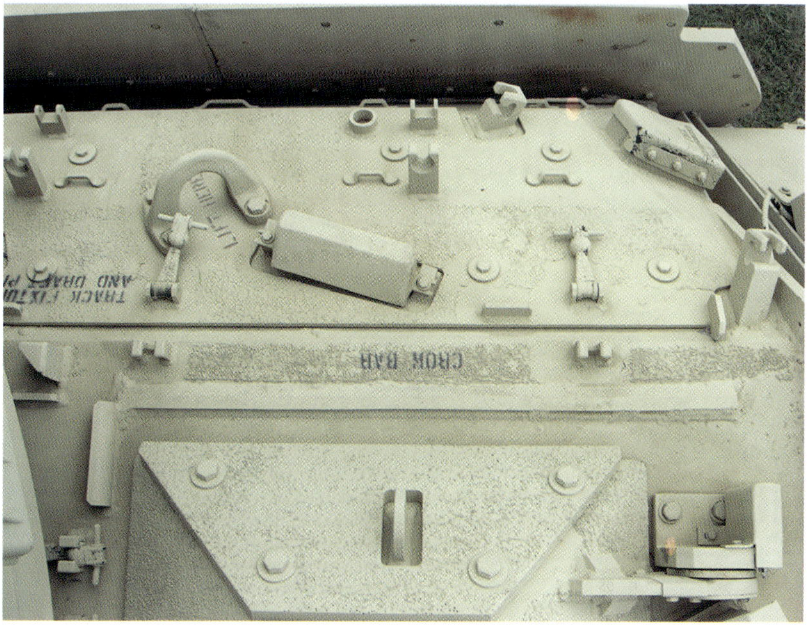

The right rear hull has brackets to mount a crow bar and a track fixture. The right side lift ring, periscope heads and fire extinguisher control are to the rear. (Gary Owsley)

The rear of the upper hull is fitted with periscopes behind the roof hatch to sight the firing port weapons. The edge of the open ramp is seen below. (Gary Owsley)

The hinges for the roof cargo hatch are at the rear. The cogged wheel allows the hatch to be raised to specific heights and still provide overhead cover, specifically for reloading the TOW launcher. (Gary Owsley)

Chapter 3

M2A3

The latest model of the Bradley is the M2A3 IFV, which entered service in 2000. The main external identifying feature is the commander's independent thermal viewer (CITV) which is mounted towards the right rear of the turret. The turret roof received additional titanium armor. The gunner's sighting system received an eye-safe laser rangefinder. The entire communication system was brought up to standards compatible with the M1A2 Abrams tank and Longbow Apache helicopter for battlefield integration. (Chris Hughes)

Above: Each of the lower spaced laminate steel armored panels that protect the suspension and lower hull is equipped with a crew step. The steps are made from lengths of cable with a solid center piece. (Chris Hughes)

Below: The last road wheel station is equipped with a shock absorber. The shock absorber attaches to the road wheel arm. An armored plate is attached to the hull floor to add further protection from mines. (Chris Hughes)

The turret is also equipped with laminate steel appliqué armor plates. The coaxial mounted 7.62mm machine gun is removed in this view. The hull front armor plates are covered in an anti-skid texture. (Chris Hughes)

The track on the Bradley is a 21 inch wide steel single pin design with a single center guide horn. The rubber contact pad can be replaced. The paint on the guide horn is worn from contact with the road wheels. (Chris Hughes)

Above: The tow lugs on the front of this M2A3 are equipped with large unpainted tow clevises. The paint is chipping from the surface of the rubber front fenders. The TOW 2 launcher has been raised to the firing position. Foot traffic has scuffed the paint on the glacis armor plate. (Chris Hughes)

Below: From lessons learned in the street fighting in Iraq the Bradley Urban Survivability Kit was developed. This included the 'dome tent' for protection of the crew from low-hanging power lines. (Chris Hughes)

The proximity of the engine exhaust to the turret produces some weathering on the turret. The dark area below the laminate armor plates is the ejection chute for spent rounds from both the main gun and the coaxial machine gun. (Chris Hughes)

The dome tent attaches to a guard for the turret-mounted antennas. The fixture, while protecting the crew, also helps to keep low-hanging wires from tangling with the antennas. The Urban Survivability kit also includes a hand-held searchlight. (Chris Hughes)

The CITV has been rotated up to its operating position. The CITV allows the commander to independently track a secondary target while the gunner engages a primary target in his ISU. (Chris Hughes)

When not in use the CITV rotates down and is protected by its armored mounting. The device allows the commander to see a target in all battlefield conditions, day, night, and through smoke, etc. (Chris Hughes)

The details of the left side of the CITV mount are seen in this rear view. The turret's rear stowage bin provides some additional stand-off armored protection for the turret rear. The bottom is perforated for drainage. (Chris Hughes)

While later models of the Bradley have the firing ports eliminated from the side armor, the rear periscopes remain. These right side periscopes are external identification of an M2 Bradley, not being present on the M3 CFV.

The rear of the upper hull mounts three periscopes for the infantry passengers. (Chris Hughes)

All of the periscopes on the M2A3 are shielded to protect the viewer's eyes from damage due to lasers used on the battlefield. The paint on the top edge of the rear troop ramp is worn. (Chris Hughes)

The rear troop ramp on the M2A3 is electro-hydraulically operated. It retains the firing ports on each side. The brackets on the right side of the ramp are for stowage of a tow cable. (Chris Hughes)

The right side firing port has a swivel mount to allow a field of fire covering the right rear corner of the vehicle. The sighting is done from the rear hull top-mounted periscopes and does not allow for precision aimed fire. (Chris Hughes)

The rear ammunition stowage lockers serve as mounts for the rear tail lights and their guards. Rubber mud flaps are mounted just below the two lockers. (Chris Hughes)

The M2A3 retains the TOW 2 armored launcher on the left side of the turret. The launcher swings upward into this raised position to prepare for firing. The TOW launcher can only be fired while the vehicle is stopped. The armored cover for the front of the launcher stays in position as the launcher rises to expose the front of the TOW tubes. (Chris Hughes)

The TOW 2 armored launcher of the M2A3 Bradley is observed in the firing position from a slightly different angle. Visible under the forward part of the launcher is the lifting cylinder. The multifaceted design of the appliqué armor on the side of the turret is evident. (Chris Hughes)

The lifting cylinder is protected by an armored cover that also pivots to depress or elevate the launcher. The TOW launcher when raised has an elevation range from +29 to -19 degrees. (Chris Hughes)

Above: The TOW launcher is lowered to a position alongside the turret when not in use. The latest improved TOW missiles are capable of penetrating over 30 inches of steel armor and are equipped with secondary warheads to defeat reactive armor. (Chris Hughes)

Opposite above: The rear of the launcher is open to allow quick reloading from the rear hull top door. The launcher is equipped with snaps on the rear edge for a protective fabric cover seen on page 67. (Chris Hughes)

Opposite below: Unlike the squad compartment of the M2A2 with its four folding seats, the M2A3 has upholstered bench seats on each side of the compartment. To the upper right are two of the three right-side periscopes, with a dome light between them. Above the front of the right seat is the squad leader's display (SLD), which provides the infantrymen in the compartment with information on the situational environment outside the vehicle. (Paul Bird)

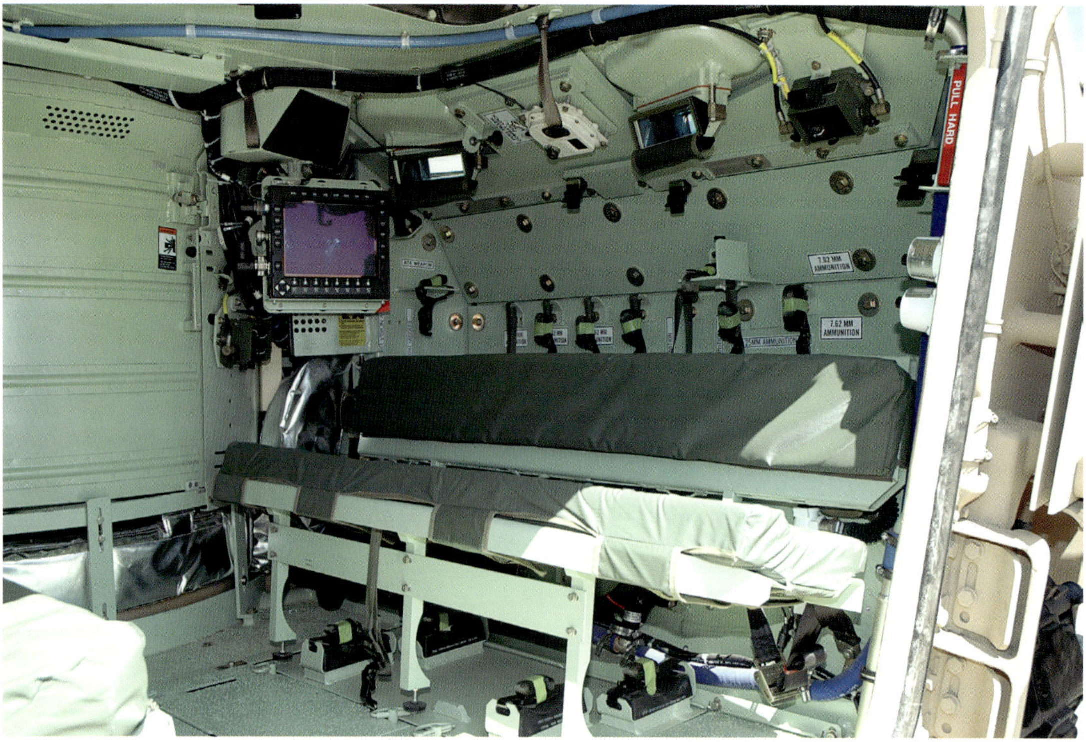
PULL HARD
7.62 MM AMMUNITION
7.62 MM AMMUNITION

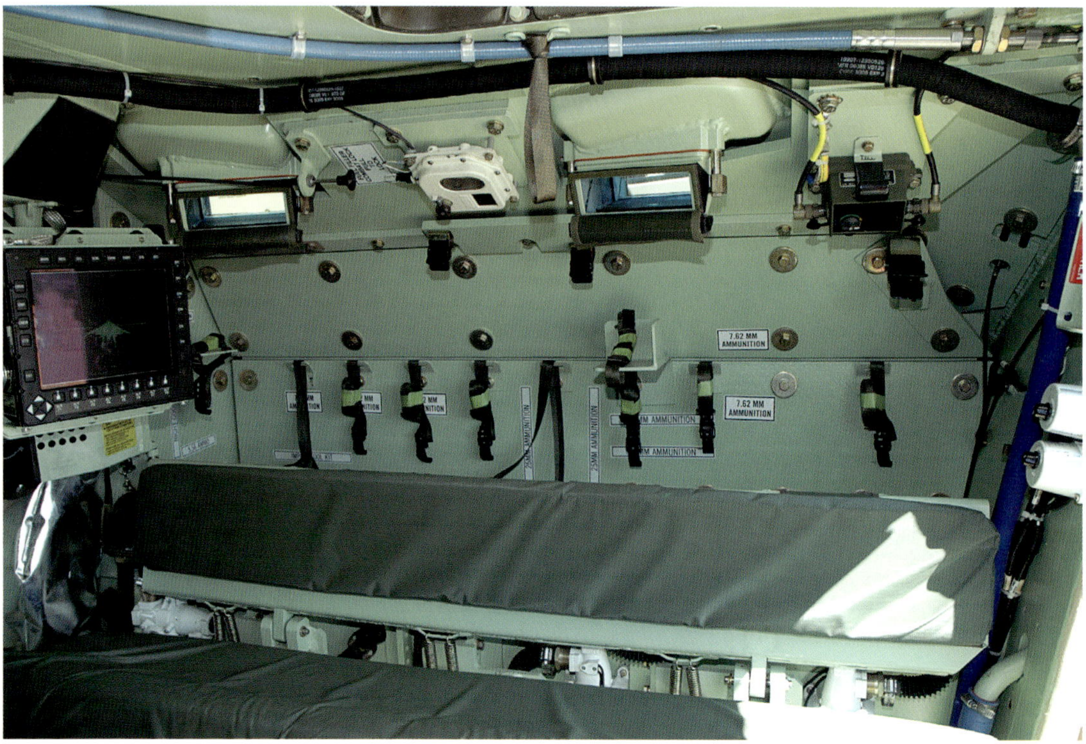
7.62 MM AMMUNITION
7.62 MM AMMUNITION

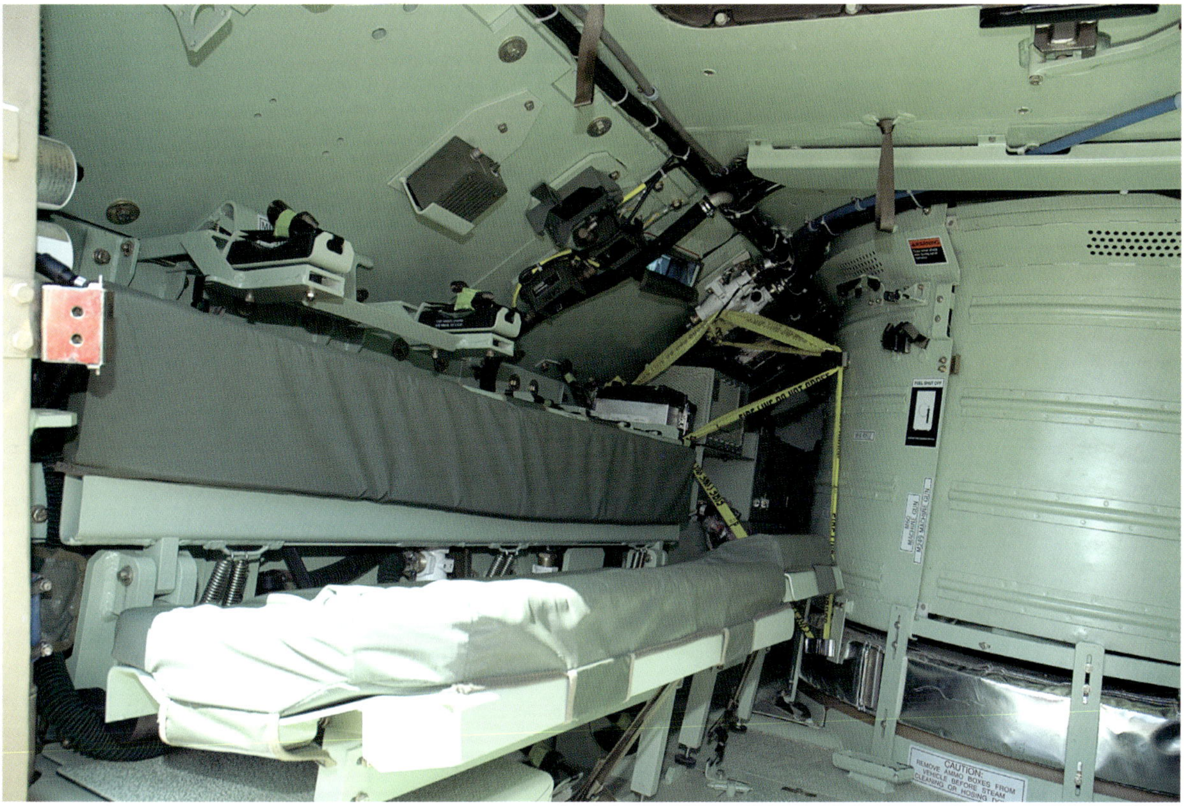

Above: In the foreground above the seat back in a view of the left side of the infantry compartment is a TOW missile storage rack. Missiles were to be stored horizontally with their noses to the rear. The olive green box above the missile rack is a loudspeaker. (Paul Bird)

Opposite above: All three periscopes on the right side of the infantry compartment are visible from this angle. Placards on the walls of the compartment indicate storage locations for items such as 7.62mm ammunition, an AT4 anti-tank weapon, and night-vision goggles. (Paul Bird)

Opposite below: The right side of the infantry compartment of an M2A3 is viewed from another angle. Olive green webbing straps with clasps, neatly bound and wrapped with light green tape, are attached with loops to the side wall; these are for strapping 7.62mm ammunition boxes in place. (Paul Bird)

The left rear corner of the infantry compartment of an M2A3 Bradley IFV is shown with the ramp lowered. Towards the upper left are two of the rear periscopes. At the top is the interior of the top hatch cover, with dark-colored weather-stripping around the bottom of the cover. The white object above the center of the photo is a dome light. (Paul Bird)

The right rear corner of the infantry compartment of an M2A3 is shown. To the top right is a rear periscope, and to the top left is the rear periscope of the right side. On the rear wall of the compartment next to the open door is a holder for a fire extinguisher. (Paul Bird)

Chapter 4

M3A3

This pair of M3A3 Bradley cavalry fighting vehicles is set up with chocks on the tracks, protective covers on the turret roof, TOW launchers, and catch pans below the final drives. The M3A3's development and external fitting parallels that of the M2A3 and entered service in 2000. The crew of the M3A3 remained five with two scouts carried in the infantry compartment and additional stowage for TOW missiles. The Dragon anti-tank missiles are replaced by the new Javelin.

The same vehicle is seen here from the front. The 25mm Bushmaster chain gun is depressed to its maximum -9 degrees, and the coax M240 machine gun has been removed.

M3A2 and M3A3 Bradleys have a different headlight arrangement than the earlier models. The heavy steel guard protects the entire light suite, which includes the lamp and amber marker light, which are standard US vehicle fittings.

The left side unit also includes a small blackout lamp in the upper right corner. The bolt heads on the back side of the hull side armor plates are visible.

Each side of the front upper hulls is fitted with a cast lifting ring which is bolted in place. This close-up provides good detail of the anti-skid texture and the back of the hull side armor.

Above: The left side lift ring is mounted outboard of the driver's hatch. The height of the driver's hatch cover in relationship to the hull is evident in this view.

Below: To the rear of the lift ring on the left front hull side is the firing handle for the vehicle's fire suppression system and storage for a spare track link.

Above: On the glacis of the M3A3, above the engine-bay cover, is an armored box with a round hole covered with a metal screen. This houses the Driver's Vision Enhancer (DVE), which provides the BFV-ODS driver the ability to operate the vehicle despite the haze of the battlefield, darkness, and adverse weather conditions. Below the hole is a flap with a leaf hinge on top.

Below: The DVE enclosure on the upper front of the hull shown in the preceding photo is viewed from above, with the front of the vehicle towards the top. To the right of it is the fluted barrel of the Bushmaster 25mm chain gun.

Above: Outboard of the main intake are the box covers for the engine exhaust and additional air intakes. These intakes feed the engine air filters. Rubber caps cover the barrels of the smoke grenade launchers.

Opposite above: The domed cover of the driver's hatch and the guard for the periscopes are also textured with the anti-skid surface. The posts on either side of the hatch protect the driver from wires strung across roads while the hatch is open.

Opposite below: The large air intake for the engine is protected by a fine wire screen. The edges of the screen are sealed to its framework by an adhesive sealer. This assembly covers the top-mounted radiator.

Above: Black rubber flaps on either side of the Bradley serve as brush guards to protect a five-gallon water can stowed behind each flap.

Opposite above: The protective box for the engine exhaust is here seen from the lower right side. The texture of the insulating material on the interior of the box is apparent. The heat of the exhaust turns the metal a rusty orange.

Opposite below: The box not only protects the exhaust opening from small arms fire, but also protects any crew on the vehicle exterior from the heat of the pipe. The thickness of the insulation is evident in this view.

Above: The line of M3A3s has been equipped with the additional turret face combat identification system panels. These plates can be attached to both sides of the turret front on the attachment points for the reactive armor boxes.

Opposite above: A section of linked rounds for the Bushmaster 25mm chain gun is laid out on the lower left corner of the engine-bay cover of a Bradley. Two of the casings are green, the others are brass. A variety of 25mm ammunition types are available, including but not limited to armor-piercing discarding-sabot, high-explosive, and practice rounds. (Paul Bird)

Opposite below: An M2A3 Bradley equipped with the additional rear antennas of a command vehicle on each rear corner of the lower hull. The extra radio equipment in these vehicles allows them to be used for command at company or brigade level.

The coaxial mounted machine gun is removed from its mount on this vehicle. The linkage for the commander's main gun sight is visible beside the 25mm Bushmaster with its clear sight ahead of his hatch. The Bushmaster is an extremely versatile weapon firing both high-explosive incendiary rounds and two types of kinetic energy penetrators to engage armored targets. The weapon is motor-driven and does not depend upon the recoil of a spent round to operate the bolt. It can fire single shots or fire automatically in two modes of 100 or 200 rounds per minute. A dual feed system has two hoppers that can supply a total of 300 ready rounds to the gun.

The sight is linked to the armored shroud at the base of the main gun and changes elevation along with the weapon. This allows the commander to roughly sight targets while operating with his head out of the hatch. The hatch has a setting that allows the commander to raise it a few inches while the cover remains horizontal. This provides him with an outside view with overhead protection.

The gun shield has a tubular armored shroud that protects the forward portion of the gun's receiver and recoil buffer assembly. The conical forward portion of the shroud is an armored casting.

The turret roof is covered by a laminate armor plate fitted around the hatch and periscopes. The fabric cover below the commander's sight keeps dust and water out of the gun mount area of the turret interior.

The commander's external sight is used in much the same way as the sight on a rifle, roughly aligning the rear sight with the cross hairs on the clear plastic plate to bring the target within view of the gunner's thermal sight.

The gunner's Integrated Sight Unit is protected by twin armored doors and an armored box on the left roof of the turret. The ISU provides 4-power or 12-power magnification of the target.

CAUTION DO NOT PUSH/PULL DOOR USE INTERNAL HANDLE ONLY
CAUTION DO NOT PUSH/PULL DOOR USE INTERNAL HANDLE ONLY

Above: This view is through an opening on the underside of the right front of the M3A3 turret. Visible inside is the receiver of the coaxial machine gun, the 7.62mm M240C. To the right is the lower left front of the turret. (Paul Bird)

Opposite above: The doors of the Integrated Sighting Unit (ISU) on an M3A3 Bradley CFV turret roof are open, allowing a view of the windows. Stenciled on the insides of the doors are warnings not to push or pull on the door but to use the internal handle only. (Paul Bird)

Opposite below: The same M3A3 turret is viewed more fully, showing the supplemental armor and other details such as the gunner's exterior sight and operating link, the coaxial machine-gun barrel, and, to the upper left, the commander's independent thermal viewer (CITV). (Paul Bird)

Above: The M3A3's CITV is stowed in a position rotated left and down to protect the optics of the system. The system provides the commander with the ability to track a secondary target independent of the gunner's primary sight.

Opposite above: The coaxial 7.62mm M240C machine gun and its mount are seen from a closer perspective. At the top is the flexible feed chute for the 7.62mm ammunition; the gun is right-hand feed. Running alongside the gun's receiver is the charging cable. (Paul Bird)

Opposite below: The turret hatches are hinged to open to the rear. The commander's hatch has a position that provides overhead protection while slightly raised. This allows the commander to safely operate with an outside view. The notches on the hinges lock the hatch lid in the various positions as it is opened. Atop the ISU is a bracket that was added for the addition of an anti-tank missile countermeasure system that was never used in service. The three tubular fittings on the rear of the ISU are for mounting range safety flags.

Above: The details of the left side of the CITV are seen in this view. The urban survivability kit mounts a 5.56mm weapon this side of the CITV that can be remotely fired on targets acquired by the commander.

Below: The rear turret bustle stowage rack provides additional spaced armor protection for the rear of the turret. The turret rear appliqué armor plates are fitted to the interior of the bustle rack.

A number of tie-down points are provided for fastening and securing the crew's personal items on the exterior of the vehicle. The interior of the vehicle can be quite cramped with its five-man crew.

Additional containers for 25mm ammunition are fixed to the rear of the turret bustle stowage rack. Storage of ammunition outside the vehicle's armor helps protect the crew from fire in the event of penetration.

Above: Details of the left rear of the turret include an additional antenna mount, a lifting ring with a corresponding cutout in the appliqué armor plate, the gunner's hatch, and the rear of the ISU with a mount for flag poles.

Opposite above: The left side of the bin is also equipped with ammunition racks. The floor of the turret bustle stowage rack is perforated to provide drainage. The global position sensor mast is seen at the right of the photo.

Opposite below: The spring base for an antenna mast is mounted at the center rear of the turret. The turret roof is coated with anti-skid texture. The tie-down points have very large areas for welding them to the surface of the vehicle.

Above: The M3A3 CFV can be identified from the rear by a lack of firing ports in the rear ramp and periscopes in the roof cargo hatch rather than the rear hull roof. The development of these vehicles paralleled that of the M2A3. The M3 Bradley was originally considered a failure in its scouting role. It was considered too large and too loud to perform the stealthy duty. The units have since changed their tactics to make the vehicle a formidable weapon. The M3s now work in concert with Abrams tanks to bring force to bear as soon as an enemy force is engaged. This is referred to as 'hunter-killer tactics'.

Opposite above: The CITV mount is provided with protective armored plate. The addition of the CITV made the act of engaging multiple targets much faster in the urban environments of Iraq.

Opposite below: The M3A3 shares the same bustle rack as the A2 variants and fits the new CITV mount.

2

2

Above: The periscopes for the two troops in the rear compartment are mounted in the roof hatch. The bustle rack is asymmetrical to clear the area behind the TOW missile launcher on the left side.

Below: The rear firing ports are not installed in the ramp of the M3 CFV series. The Bradley did not initially fit the cavalry's idea of a scout vehicle. They are now used in conjunction with the Abrams in hunter-killer teams.

The cargo hatch cover of the M3 differs greatly from that of the M2. The hatch is made from a stamped armor plate with the appliqué plates specifically designed to fit the hatch contours.

The armored skirt protecting the rear idler is in its raised position. There is a crew step on the inside of the skirt as well as the outside. The huge shock absorber for the last road wheel station is visible behind the idler wheel.

Above: The road wheel at the first right hand road wheel station carries a 24x4 inch rubber tire. The hub on later variant wheels has a clear lubrication sight glass to aid in keeping up with maintenance.

Below: The drive sprocket has two forged eleven-tooth rings bolted to a central cast hub. The pitch diameter is 21 inches. The rubber contact portion of the track is visible.

A track on an M3A3 Bradley CFV is viewed from the front, with the right final-drive housing to the right of the photo. The Bradley tracks are a single-pin, center-guide design, made of steel with replaceable rubber shoes. Each link is 21 inches wide, with a pitch (front-to-rear length) of six inches. (Paul Bird)

A motorized actuator raises the heavy armored engine bay cover to expose the power train within. The front of the compartment is occupied by the HMPT-500-3 automatic transmission.

CAUTION

Right: The driver's position of the M3A3 is identical to that seen earlier in the M2A2. The steering yoke controls the speed of the left and right track to steer the vehicle. The brake and accelerator pedals are below the yoke.

Opposite above: The Cummins VTA-903T Diesel engine is a turbocharged V-8 displacing 903 cubic inches (14.8 liters). Rated at 600 hp, it provides excellent performance with a top speed of 35 mph on paved roads.

Opposite below: The engine bay of an M3A3, also called the power-unit compartment, is viewed from the left front of the vehicle. To compensate for the increased weight of the M3A3, in addition to the increased-horsepower Cummins VTA-903T engine, an improved transmission, the HMPT-500-3EC, was used. (Paul Bird)

Above: Interesting details are seen on this repainted M3A3 Bradley CFV. In the first Gulf War it was common to see European paint below the hastily painted sand-colored finishes. Here we see the reverse.

Below: The driver's Combat Vehicle Crew (CVC) helmet is placed on the left side wire cutter beside his open hatch. The CVC is equipped with earphones and a mic; the driver's yoke has a push-to-talk button built in to ease communication.

The driver's hatch of an M3A3 Bradley CFV and a CVC helmet are viewed from the left side of the vehicle. The glass of the periscope objectives exhibits different colors, such as the lavender and reddish hues seen here, depending on the light. (Paul Bird)

The driver's compartment of an M3A3 Bradley is viewed through the roof looking to the rear. In the foreground on the engine-compartment bulkhead is a placard with detailed operating instructions for the vehicle. Below the placard is a holder for an M16 rifle butt. On the access door aft of the placard is a holder for gun tools and spare parts. In the foreground is the driver's seat, with the seat back folded down at the center of the photo. (Paul Bird)

HORN
TURN INDICATOR
TURRET POWER
LAUNCHER UP
km/h
TRANS OIL PRESS
TRANS OIL TEMP
FUEL FILTER CLOGGED
RAMP
STARTER CUTOUT OVERRIDE
COLD START
MASTER POWER
ENGINE ACCESSORY
THROTTLE
DRIVER'S VISION ENHANCER
CAUTION
SHIFT PATTERN

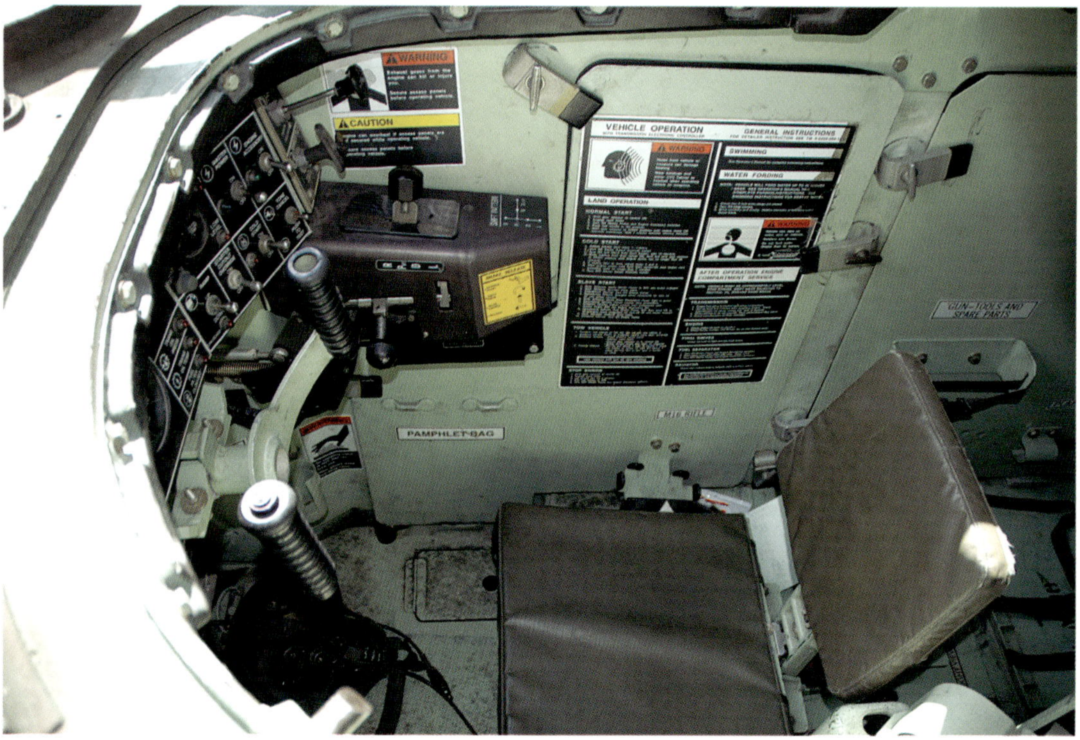

WARNING
CAUTION
VEHICLE OPERATION
GENERAL INSTRUCTIONS
LAND OPERATION
SWIMMING
WATER FORDING
PAMPHLET BAG
GUN-TOOLS AND SPARE PARTS

Above: The left side of the M3A3 driver's compartment is viewed through the driver's hatch. The box at the center of the photo is assumed to be an indicator for the onboard navigation system. The black box at the top left is the heater control. To the left is the driver's seat support. (Paul Bird)

Opposite above: The driver's steering yoke and instrument panel are viewed from above the driver's hatch. At the center of the panel is the speedometer, with gauges in miles per hour and kilometers per hour. The green fixture on the far left of the panel contains the light switches. To the right of these switches are the horn and turn-indicator controls. On the right side of the panel are the ramp switch, master power and engine accessory switches, engine coolant temperature gauge, and other switches. (Paul Bird)

Opposite below: On the right side of the driver's compartment to the rear of the instrument panel is the transmission gear selector. On the top of the selector housing is marked the shift pattern. On the side of the selector housing are the control for releasing the brakes and a placard with instructions on releasing the brakes. (Paul Bird)

PULL HARD

Above: Much of the squad compartment of an M3A3 Bradley CFV is viewed through the rear door. At the center background is the rear of the shield for the turret basket, with the crew access door open. To the left of the door is the squad leader's display. On the right sidewall are missile storage racks. On the crew seat to the left is a TOW missile storage/launching tube. (Paul Bird)

Opposite above: The M3A3 Bradley cavalry fighting vehicle differs from the Bradley infantry fighting vehicle in that the former has three periscopes in the roof hatch cover over the squad compartment. The hatch cover is viewed from the left side; the hinges are on the rear of the cover. On the interior of the cover is a handle. (Paul Bird)

Opposite below: In this view, taken through the top hatch of the squad compartment of an M3A3 Bradley CFV, part of the right sidewall is visible, including, at the center, a missile storage rack, with red cushions and an olive green webbing strap for securing the missiles in place. (Paul Bird)

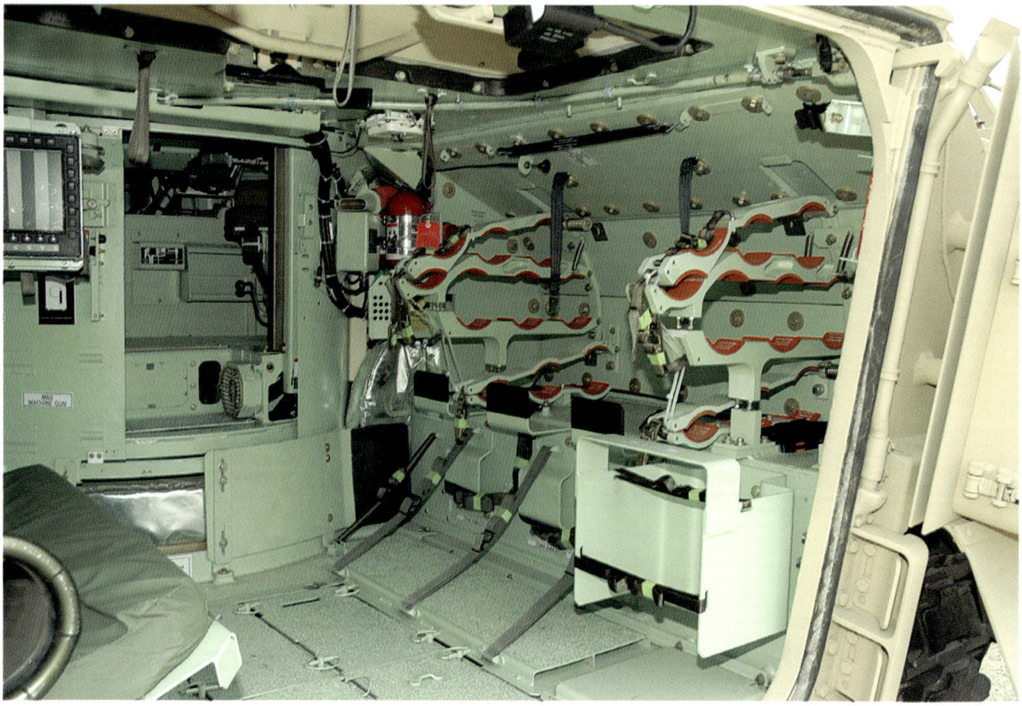

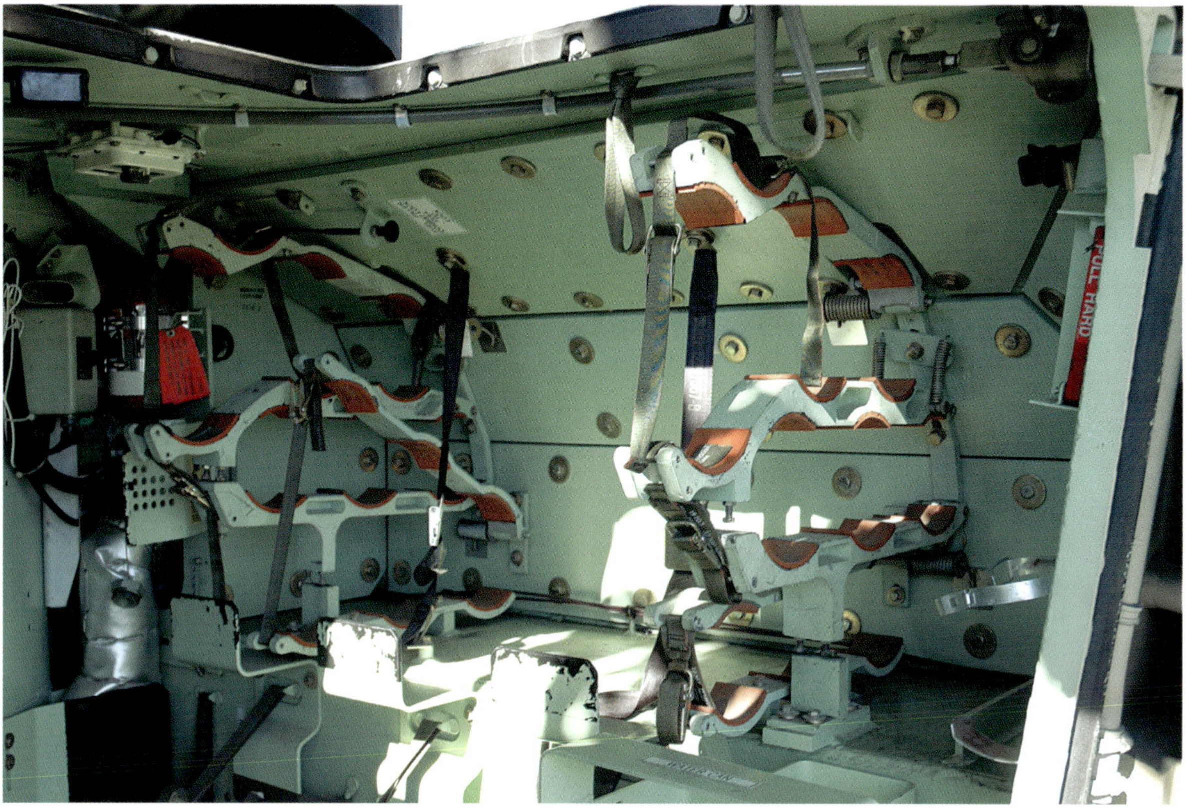

Above: The storage racks for the ten TOW 2 missile tubes are in the right rear of the crew compartment. The segments of the spall liner can be seen on the hull side behind the missile stowage racks.

Opposite above: The squad compartment of an M3A3 Bradley CFV is viewed through the rear entry. At the center is the rear of the turret-basket shield, with the sliding crew-access door open. On the left side of the enclosure is the squad leader's display, part of the A3 Bradley's sophisticated system for enhancing the situational awareness of the crew. (Paul Bird)

Opposite below: The right side of the squad compartment of the M3A3 is mainly dedicated to storage facilities for the TOW missiles and 25mm ammunition. The white structure to the lower right is a storage rack for a water can. To the front of that rack are storage points for 25mm ammunition boxes. Note the pebbly, non-slip surface on the floor panels.

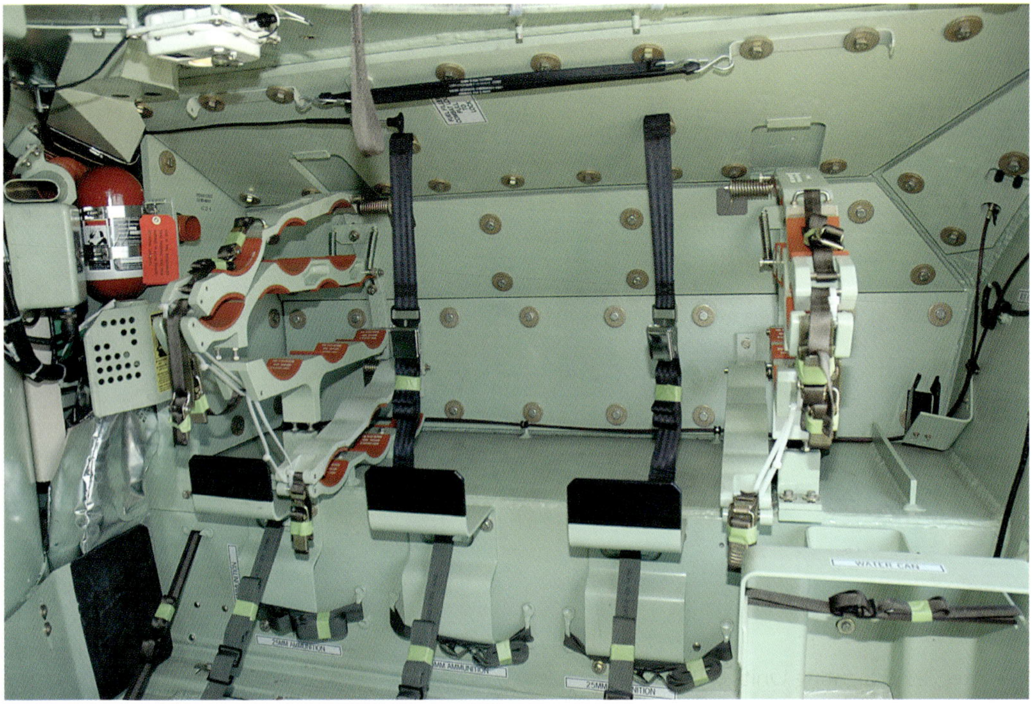

The racks for ten TOW missiles are of a clamping design and comprise ten principal sections, five forward and five rear. The bottom tier of three missiles is cradled in top and bottom clamps with red cushions. The next tier up has top and bottom clamps for three TOW missiles. The top clamp of that tier also forms the bottom clamp of an upper tier of three missiles, and on top of the upper clamps for that tier are cradles for one more missile, to be secured in place by the webbing straps seen here. (Paul Bird)

The commander's station in the turret of the M3A3 is viewed from below, with his seat at the bottom. At the center of the photo is the commander's flat-panel display. Above the seat is a sliding tray for a keyboard. To the top of the photo is the commander's open hatch. (Paul Bird)

The gunner's station in the M3A3 turret is viewed through the crew-access door in the rear of the turret basket. Towards the lower left, above and to the front of the seat, are flexible feed chutes for ammunition. Above the chutes are the gunner's hand controls, with dual grips to allow the gunner to use either hand to traverse, elevate, and fire the chain gun, the coaxial machine gun, and the TOW launcher.

The gunner's (left) and the commander's (right) stations are visible in this photo. On the Integrated Sighting Unit to the left, the left eyepiece is for the night scope and the right eyepiece is for the day scope. The receiver of the 25mm chain gun is forward of the perforated housing at the center.

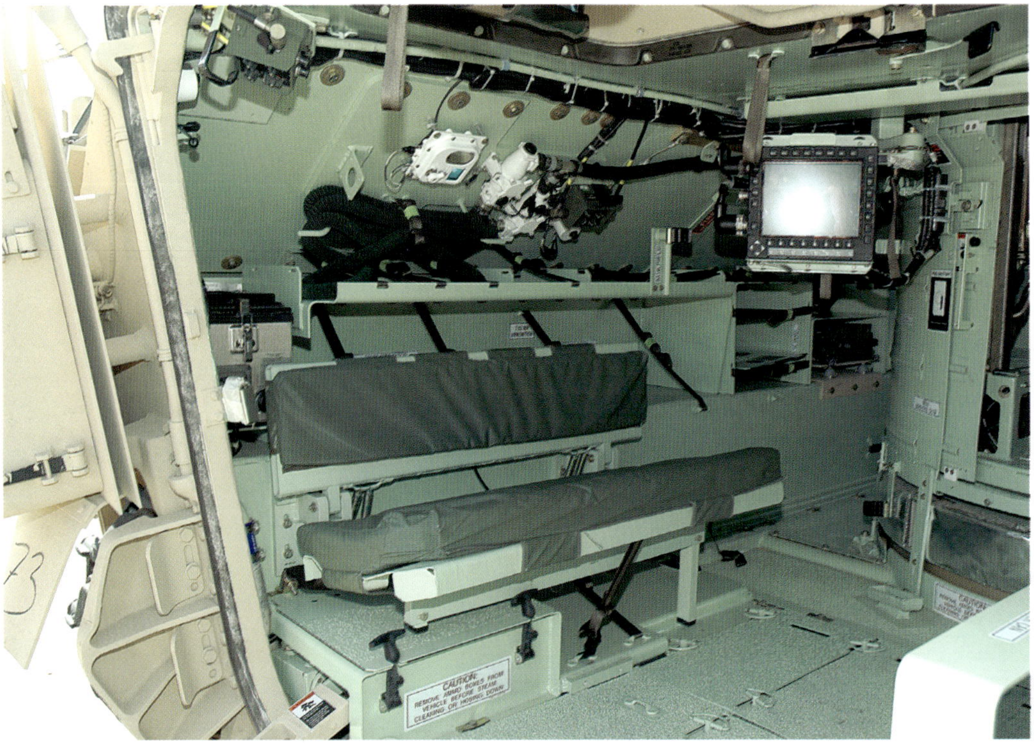
CAUTION:
REMOVE AMMO BOXES FROM
VEHICLE BEFORE STEAM
CLEANING OR HOSING DOWN

Above: The flat panel display screen in the commander's station is new to the A3 series. With this screen he can send and receive messages via the Army's wireless digital communications system known as FBCB2.

Opposite above: Whereas the M3(A0) – the first-generation Bradley CFV – had two folding crew seats in the middle of the floor of the crew compartment, the M3A3 Bradley CFV has a single folding bench seat on the left side of the compartment, making for freer movement inside the compartment. (Paul Bird)

Opposite below: Looking left across the turret into the gunner's position, the gunner's ISU and hand controls are to the right of the picture. The breech assembly of the gun does not enter into the turret crew's area.

Chapter 5

The M270 Multiple Launch Rocket System

The chassis of the Bradley was lengthened to form the basis of the Multiple Launch Rocket System. This chassis was known as the M993 Multiple Launch Rocket System carrier. Upon this chassis was mounted the M270 ground vehicle mounted rocket launcher. The launcher housed two rocket pods, each of which were loaded with six 227mm M26 rockets. These rockets could be fired one at a time or in rapid sequence. The M26 rocket has a range of 32 kilometers, and carries 644 M77 submunitions each. A three-man crew consisting of driver, gunner, and section leader served the weapon system.

The only variant chassis to be developed from the Bradley fighting vehicle chassis has been the M933 carrier, an extended chassis with a front cab of aluminum-alloy armor. Several special-purpose prototype or experimental vehicles based on the M933 have been built, with only two models going into production and being accepted by the army: the M4 command-and-control vehicle, of which 25 units were built; and the M270 MLRS, as seen here. (Paul Bird)

Above: The three louvered shutters over the windshields of the cab of an M270 MLRS are viewed close-up. The slats are of pivoting design and can be opened to allow the occupants of the cab a forward view without raising the entire shutter assemblies, which are hinged at the top for the driver's assembly and the bottom for the others. (Paul Bird)

Below: The cab of an M270 MLRS is viewed from the front left corner. The platform vehicle that supports the M270 MLRS is the M993 Carrier Vehicle, an elongated derivative of the Bradley fighting vehicle. The personnel doors of the cab have a hinged, ballistic window with a vision block.

DO NOT
FORKLIFT AREA

Above: The turret is viewed from its left side, with the right elevation actuator support in the background. Prominent inside the turret is the elevation transmission; the mechanism with a slightly bent shape attached to the elevation transmission is the elevation servo-motor assembly.

Opposite above: The M269 loader-launcher module (LLM), also known as the cage, is elevated, showing details of its lower side. The inner struts are the elevation actuator supports. The outer pair of struts are jury struts, which are installed when the launcher is to be left elevated, to help support it.

Opposite below: With the rocket launcher elevated, a view of the turret, on which the cage is mounted, is provided. To the far right is the hydraulic power supply. In the center foreground is the elevation transmission. Also in view are other mechanisms for elevating and traversing the launcher.

Above: The beam structure projecting from the upper front of the cage of the MLRS is a telescoping boom with an integrated winch for loading pods containing the rockets into the launcher. The MLRS receives reloads of rockets from the M270 MLRS Self-Propelled Loader/Launcher (SPLL).

Opposite above: The outer left side of the turret is at the bottom of the photo. Two pivot fittings on the bottom rear of the cage are pinned to two sets of pivot lugs on the rear of the turret; these fittings provide the pivot points for elevating and depressing the cage. The left pivot fitting is visible to the right.

Opposite below: A composite light is in a recess on each side of the rear bumper. The small latch to the right of the light is for the cover of a stowage compartment for a track-connecting fixture, drift pin, ax, crowbar, sledgehammer, and grease gun. At the top right is the bottom of the left jury strut.

Above: The left hoist motor and cable drum are seen from underneath, with the left outer rail of the boom assembly in the foreground. (Paul Bird)

Opposite above: The extended boom of an MLRS is viewed from the right side. Mounted on cross-beams at the center of the boom are two hoist motors, each of which drives a hoist cable drum. The hoist cables are routed through a series of pulleys mounted on the two hoist-pulley support assemblies, the frame-type structures to the front of the motors, from which the cables pass downward. (Paul Bird)

Opposite below: The left hoist-pulley support assembly is viewed from below, with the front of the boom to the left of the photo. (Paul Bird)

Above: The rear part of the extended boom is seen from below the left side. Note the rollers on which the rails of the boom ride when being extended and retracted. The interior of the cage, where two rocket pods would be loaded, is visible. (Paul Bird)

Opposite above: The rear of the cage of an M270 MLRS is shown without the rocket pods loaded. The cage is traversed to the right. The pivots on which the cage is elevated and depressed are at the lower outside corners of the cage. (Paul Bird)

Opposite below: Hoist hooks from an MLRS boom are attached to two six-pack launcher pods. The M270 MLRS is able to fire a variety of rocket types of the MLRS Family of Munition (MFOM). The M270 also is capable of firing the Army Tactical Missile System (ATACMS), a large guided missile capable of delivering a variety of warheads. Two ATACMS can be loaded into the cage at a time. (Paul Bird)

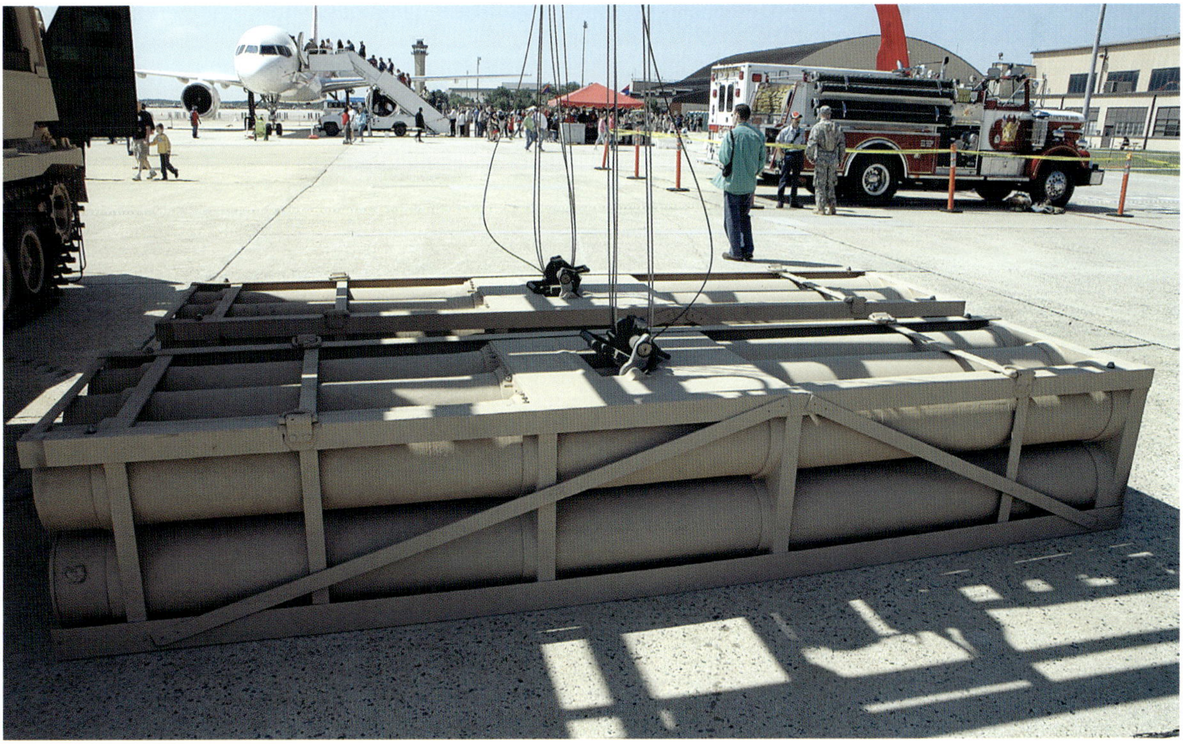

Above: The rear of the loader-launcher module is exhibited. Twelve launch tubes are positioned in two rocket pods; six rockets are mounted in each pod. This example is an M270A1 MLRS, similar to the M270 but with improved fire control and launcher mechanical systems.

Below: Recessed into the bottom right of the rear bumper/stowage box is a trailer receptacle. A tow pintle is at the lower center of the vehicle's hull, and small clamps and two curved brackets for holding a tow cable in place are also arranged on the lower rear plate of the hull.

Above: To the left is the left pivot fitting on the bottom rear of the loader-launcher module, or cage, as well as the two pivot lugs to which the pivot is pinned. Above the pivot on the rear of the loader-launcher module is a hinged door providing access to the boom controller and a storage box.

Below: The full extent of the frame member on the right side of the turret of the M270 MLRS is exhibited. The circular bay containing the elevation transmission and servo, the hydraulic power supply, and other components is visible in the center of the turret. In the foreground is the right fender.

The right side of the engine compartment is viewed close-up. The prominent, louvered feature on the side of the compartment is the engine and coolant air exhaust grille. On top of the compartment, but out of view, are the engine air intake and the engine air intake grille.

In a partial view of the left side of an M270 MLRS, the loader-launcher module is traversed to the right, and the rear of the LLM is to the right. The launcher tubes have been removed from the LLM. To the left is the engine compartment, situated to the rear of the cab. Note the large and small access doors on the side of the compartment. (Paul Bird)

Above: An M270 MLRS painted in NATO woodland camouflage is on display. The louvers on the left and center windshield covers are open, while those on the right cover are closed. The vehicle is marked for Battery B, 6th Field Artillery Regiment. Jutting from the front of the loader-launcher module is the telescoping boom. (Paul Bird)

Below: The loader-launcher module is traversed to the left on this M270 MLRS. The missiles to the front of the launcher are from a separate display. The louvers on the armored shutter over the driver's window are closed, while those on the gunner's (center) and commander's windows are open.

Above: The sprocket wheels are at the front of the suspension; this is the left one. The manufacturer's and part numbers are embossed on the inner rim. Also visible on the end of each track link is a track link nut, which secures the track pin. The tracks are 21 inches wide with a 6 inch pitch. (Paul Bird)

Opposite above: The M270 MLRS has six dual road wheels per side, with 24x4 inch rubber tires, and are mounted on torsion bars. Supporting the upper run of track on each side are two single return rollers (one is visible at the left) and two dual return rollers (one is at the right). (Paul Bird)

Opposite below: Part of the suspension on the left side of a M270 MLRS is displayed, including four of the bogie-wheel assemblies and two of the track-support rollers, which are dual-wheel units with a relatively large diameter. Rubber tires are fitted to both types of wheels. Also visible are the upper ends of the bogie arms. Note how the paint has been rubbed off the guide horns of the tracks. (Paul Bird)

A dual adjustable idler is at the rear of each side of the suspension; the left one is depicted. Shock absorbers are provided for the first two road wheels and the last road wheel on each side; the rear one is visible between the idler and the road wheel. The tracks are center-guide. (Paul Bird)

The right, or commander's, door, like the driver's door, has a ballistic window that incorporates an armored glass vision block and hinges with a torsion bar. The top door hinge is to the right. The cab is constructed of 7039 aluminum armor, while the body is made of 5083 aluminum armor. (Paul Bird)

The inside of the driver's door is shown with the blackout cover in the lowered position, showing the glass vision block. This block is on a window panel that can be opened; the latch handle for the panel is at the top. The green sign warns that the window is spring-loaded and slams shut when its handle is released. (Paul Bird)

The interior of an MLRS carrier cab is seen through the driver's door. Seats are provided for the three-man crew: the driver, the gunner, and in the far seat, the section chief, or commander. The small crew is made possible by the computerized fire-control system and the well-designed mechanicals. (Paul Bird)

The ceiling of the cab is viewed through the commander's door, facing towards the rear. Directly above the commander's seat is an intercom control box; a dome light is adjacent to the left rear corner of the commander's hatch. Behind the seats are shelves for equipment.

The commander's door is open, showing his seat, a map board on the front of the cab, and some details of the interior of the door. A hinged blackout cover is in the raised position on the vision block on the door. A bit of the commander's open hatch in the roof of the cab is visible.

Details of the cab interior above the windshields are seen from the section chief's seat. To the left of the grab handle are the control handles for the left and center louvers; the control handle for the right louvers is to the far right. Next to it is a caution sign that the crew must wear both headphones and earplugs when operating the vehicle; this is because of the danger of hearing loss or damage from the constant noise in the cab. (Paul Bird)

In front of the steering yoke is the instrument panel, to the right of which are the slo-pump handle, for locking out the suspension system, and the gunner's control panel. The red object just inside the door is the engine compartment fire extinguisher, with a manual control knob.

Above: As seen through the driver's door, the box on the ceiling between the dome lights has a ventilation fan switch. Data plates and informational placards are arrayed on the ceiling and front of the cab. Above where the two windows meet are louver-control handles.

Opposite above: A US Army M270 MLRS launches a rocket. This system can 'shoot' a load of 12 rockets in less than one minute and then 'scoot' away to a new position before the enemy can establish the MLRS's position and retaliate. It can hit targets up to 26 miles away, or, when the ATACMS missile is fired from the M270, up to 190 miles away. (DoD)

Opposite below: Although it scarcely resembles the fighting vehicles, the M270 and M270A1 Multiple Launch Rocket Systems are considered a part of the Bradley family. The vehicles share many of the driveline and suspension components, which is what causes both the army and the manufacturer to group these vehicles with the Bradley. Here, an M270 launches a rocket at White Sands Missile Range. (US Army)

Chapter 6

The Bradley Deployed

At the heart of the Bradley fighting vehicle's offensive and defensive weapons was the BGM-71 TOW (Tube-launched, Optically-tracked, Wire-guided) anti-tank missile. This missile entered service during the Vietnam war and has been upgraded since. It has an operational range of almost three miles and can penetrate vertical armor seventeen inches thick. Seen here is a BGM-71D TOW 2 missile, with a distinctive probe on the nose, which has just been fired from the twin-tube launcher of an M2A1 Bradley. (DoD)

The fighting-vehicles program that included the M2 and M3 Bradley was extended in 1979 to include a general-support rocket-system carrier; this went into production as the M270 Multiple Launch Rocket System (MLRS) Self-Propelled Launcher Loader (SPLL). This potent, highly effective weapon system was based on a carrier derived from the Bradley chassis and drive train and could fire twelve 227mm guided or unguided rockets to a range of twenty-six miles. The MLRS first saw combat in Operation Desert Storm in 1991. (DoD)

This photo and the following series of images document M2 Bradley infantry fighting vehicles, demonstrating their amphibious capabilities on Victory Pond, Fort Benning, Georgia, on 13 June 1983. For operations on water, the trim vane on the glacis was swung forward and secured, and the water barrier around the sides and rear of the hull were deployed, as seen here. (DoD)

Above: Propelled by its tracks, an M2 Bradley chugs across the pond. The Bradley is able to reach a speed of about 4.5 miles per hour in the water. (DoD)

Below: An M2 Bradley is viewed from the left rear while crossing Victory Pond. Both the driver's hatch (to the rear of the trim vane) and the cargo hatch (the GI to the right is leaning on it) are open. (DoD)

Above: The waterline is evident in the form of the wet area of the water barrier on an M2 Bradley infantry fighting vehicle emerging from Victory Pond. Note the two rigging lines attached to the trim vane. (DoD)

Below: Water drains from the spaces above the tracks on an M2 Bradley as it departs from Victory Pond. The Bradley is able to ford water up to 3.5 feet in depth without the water barrier and trim vane erected. (DoD)

Above: An M2 Bradley, likely the same one as in the preceding photo, of 3rd Platoon, E Troop, 2nd Battalion, 6th Cavalry, is viewed from the right rear with the ramp lowered during a training exercise at the US Army Armor Center, Fort Knox, during 1983. Just inside the vehicle on the center of the floor are two folding crew seats. The two firing ports on each side of the exterior of the fighting compartment, and the three periscopes on the hull roof to the rear of the cargo hatch, were not present on the M3 Bradley. (DoD)

Opposite above: In addition to the twin BGM-71 TOW launcher on the left side of the turret of the M2 Bradley infantry fighting vehicle, the M2 also is armed with a turret-mounted M242 Bushmaster 25mm chain gun. It is a chain-driven automatic cannon, with a variable rate of fire of 200 or 500 rounds per minute, an effective range of 9,800 feet and maximum range of 22,300 feet. In this image, an infantryman is inspecting the M242 on an M2 Bradley. (DoD)

Opposite below: Members of the 3rd Platoon, E Troop, 2nd Battalion, 6th Cavalry, go about their duties while operating an M2 Bradley infantry fighting vehicle during maneuvers at the US Army Armor Center in 1983. The vehicle is painted in MERDC camouflage; it appears to be the Summer, US and Europe, Verdant version, consisting of Forest Green, Light Green, Sand, and Black. (DoD)

Above: A Bradley advances along a swale during maneuvers at Fort Knox in 1983. The TOW launcher on the left side of the turret is in its travel position; preparatory to firing, the launcher was swung upwards ninety degrees. The box-shaped object with an open flap on the outboard side is the housing of the Integrated Sight Unit (ISU), equipped with a day sight and a night sight for use by the gunner and the commander. (DoD)

Opposite above: An M2 Bradley crewman from Scout Platoon, Headquarters and Headquarters Company, 3rd Battalion, 67th Armor, removes bolts from the access plate for the left final drive during Spearpoint '84, a phase of Exercise Reforger '84, in August 1984. Inside the vehicle is the Cummins VTA-903T V-8, 4-cycle, 903 cubic inch, turbosupercharged engine. (DoD)

Opposite below: The first M2 Bradley Infantry Fighting vehicle to be drawn from a Prepositioning of Material Configured to Unit Sets (POMCUS) site is departing from a warehouse in West Germany in August 1984. POMCUS was a program for stockpiling US military equipment in West Germany, for rapid deployment in the event of war with the Soviet Union. This M2 was being moved out for participation in the Spearpoint '84 phase of Exercise Reforger '84. On this vehicle the M242 Bushmaster 25mm chain gun has not yet been remounted. (DoD)

An M2 Bradley infantry fighting vehicle, with service headlights on, is in the background as Sergeant Larry Hersch, 7th Infantry, provides security for an armored column advancing through Langgöns, West Germany, during the Central Guardian phase of Reforger '85. (DoD)

The rear section of armored skirt is secured in the raised position on an M2 Bradley while members of a squad enter the vehicle during Exercise Reforger '85. Note the dust cover over the rear of the TOW missile launcher, the tail lights on the two rear storage boxes, and the detachable beacon on the brush guard of the left tail light. (DoD)

Above: An M2 Bradley IFV is being refueled in the field from a tanker with a trailer holding a tank or bladder during exercise Reforger '85. A windscreen with three soft-plastic windows has been erected in front of the driver's hatch. Armor for the M2 included a mix of spaced-laminate armor, 5083 aluminum armor, and 7039 aluminum armor. (DoD)

Below: During the Cold War, the Multiple Integrated Laser Engagement System (MILES) was devised to simulate actual combat with vehicle-mounted weapons, using laser, sensors, and other equipment to replicate the effects of firing and hits. This M2 Bradley of 2nd Battalion, 41st Infantry, 2nd Armored Division, is equipped with MILES during maneuvers at the Antelope Mound training area, Fort Hood, Texas, in January 1986. This includes, on the chain gun barrel, a Flash Weapon Effect Signature Simulator (FLASHWESS). The light with an amber dome on top of the turret is also part of MILES and is called the CVKI light; it was used to signal hits, kills, and near misses. (DoD)

Above: Heavily festooned with tree branches for local-camouflage purposes, and equipped with MILES, three M2 Bradley infantry fighting vehicles from the 2nd Battalion, 41st Infantry, 2nd Armored Division, stand by after a company team attack exercise with M1 Abrams main battle tanks at the Shell Point training area at Fort Hood, Texas, in January 1986. The nickname 'DEATH DEALER' is stenciled in black on the front of the turret of the closest M2. (DoD)

Opposite above: During training maneuvers of the 2nd Battalion, 41st Infantry, 2nd Armored Division, an M2 Bradley advances out of a thicket as part of a company team attack exercise at Antelope Mound, Fort Hood, in January 1986. A CVKI light is visible above the turret roof. (DoD)

Opposite below: An M3 Bradley advances through a village during the spring or summer portion of Exercise Reforger '85. To each side of the gun mantlet on the turret are M257 smoke grenade launchers, each with four launcher tubes, above which is a storage box for extra smoke grenades. The coaxial 7.62mm M240C machine gun on the right-hand side of the 25mm M242 gun has been dismounted. (DoD)

BRADLEY
US ARMY
MV0020

Above: United States and Jordanian military officers inspect three M2 Bradley infantry fighting vehicles (left, and right background) and a then-new M1A1 Abrams main battle bank (right) during the capabilities-exercise portion of Exercise Shadow Hawk '87. The purpose of this exercise, part of Exercise Bright Star '87, was to evaluate procedures used to deploy US tactical and logistical forces to the Middle East. (DoD)

Opposite above: Three M2 Bradley infantry fighting vehicles loaded on tank transporters are on a pier at the Port of Aqaba in Jordan. The vehicles, painted in desert camouflage, were being transported to Egypt at the conclusion of Exercise Shadow Hawk, a phase of Exercise Bright Star '87. A clear view is available of the early-production turret bustle storage bin, the rear of which slanted forwards at the top. (DoD)

Opposite below: During the capabilities-exercise phase of Exercise Shadow Hawk in September 1987, the commander, loader, and driver of an M2 Bradley are visible in their hatches. The inverted-V shape to the rear of the 25mm gun is the support for an external ring sight for the commander's use. Stenciled to the rear of the registration number on the hull is a crest marked 'BRADLEY' over a crossed rifle and sword and five stars. (DoD)

Above: Soldiers from a Stinger man-portable anti-aircraft missile unit wearing MILES gear are advancing along a road as an M2 Bradley passes by at the National Training Center, Fort Irwin, California. The M2 has unit markings on the final-drive housings for the 33rd vehicle in the line of march of Company C, 2nd Battalion, 24th Infantry Division (Mechanized). Coils of barbed wire are stored on the side of the hull. (DoD)

Opposite above: An M2 Bradley infantry fighting vehicle of the 24th Infantry Division (Mechanized), apparently the same vehicle depicted in the preceding photo, advances with turret traversed to the left rear during an exercise at the National Training Center. Individual crew packs are stowed on the rear of the turret, and rations boxes and other gear are on the trim vane. (DoD)

Opposite below: Major General Thomas P. Carney, commander of the 5th Infantry Division (Mechanized), is about to christen an M3 Bradley cavalry fighting vehicle with a bottle of champagne during a ceremony celebrating its arrival at Fort Polk, Louisiana, in April 1990. The M3 has unit markings for the 3rd Squadron, 1st Cavalry Regiment, 5th Infantry Division (Mech.). (DoD)

HQ-66

Above: The trim vane has been lowered and the engine-compartment hatch opened on an M3 Bradley cavalry fighting vehicle, assigned to the 3rd Squadron, 1st Cavalry Regiment, 5th Infantry Division (Mechanized) at Fort Polk, Louisiana, in April 1990. From this angle, the M3 was similar in appearance to the M2 Bradley infantry fighting vehicle, the main differences being on the rear half of the exteriors and in the interior of the vehicles. (DoD)

Opposite above: An interior view through the rear hatch of an M3 Bradley cavalry fighting vehicle assigned to the 3rd Squadron, 1st Cavalry Regiment, reveals the two back-to-back, folding crew seats in the center foreground and storage racks for TOW missiles to the right. In the center background is the turret basket and its entry hatch. Since there were only two men in the rear compartment of the M3, exclusive of the turret, as opposed to six men in the M2, the M3 had much more space for ammunition storage. (DoD)

Opposite below: In 1990 and 1991 the Bradley fighting vehicles went to war, as Coalition armed forces concentrated in Saudi Arabia to prepare for ejecting Iraqi forces from Kuwait. Here, Bradleys of L Troop, 3rd Armored Cavalry Regiment, are at a depot during Operation Desert Shield, the buildup phase of the campaign. The nickname 'LAWRENCE' is stenciled above a crossed-sabre emblem on the hull of the first vehicle, an M3 cavalry fighting vehicle, above the black and white diamond-shaped tactical symbol. Notice the blanked-out firing ports and lack of periscopes on the hull side. (DoD)

V

24-3-151

Above: A videographer from a combat pictorial team shoots footage of an M2 Bradley infantry fighting vehicle of the 24th Infantry Division (Mechanized) as it arrives at an encampment during Operation Desert Shield in January 1991. The turret is traversed to the left, and the TOW missile launcher is in firing position. (DoD)

Opposite above: Members of the 24th Infantry Division (Mechanized) have just erected a camouflage net over their M2 Bradley infantry fighting vehicle at an encampment in Saudi Arabia during Operation Desert Shield in January 1991. On the hull below the black V for Victory divisional symbol on the TOW launcher are stenciled in black the names of two crewmen and the nickname of the vehicle, 'The Destroyer'. (DoD)

Opposite below: In a view of an M2 Bradley, possibly the same one in the preceding image, under camouflage netting at an encampment in Saudi Arabia in January 1991, unit markings for the 3rd Battalion, 15th Infantry Regiment, 24th Infantry Division (Mechanized) are on the door of the left rear storage box. On the lowered ramp, to the left, is an oblong crew door, for entering or exiting the vehicle without lowering the ramp. On the door and to the right of it are round access doors for the rear firing ports. Towards the left bottom of the ramp is its operating arm. (DoD)

WALL DRUG
7544 MILES

Above: 'The Destroyer', an M2 Bradley from the 24th Infantry Division (Mechanized), seen in a preceding photograph, has arrived at a camp in Saudi Arabia during Operation Desert Shield. A coil of barbed wire is secured to the trim vane, for use in defensive works while encamping. (DoD)

Opposite above: In a humorous vein, during Operation Desert Shield in January 1990 two soldiers stand next to an M3 Bradley with a sign mimicking the ubiquitous highway billboards seen in the western states, advertising a certain tourist attraction in South Dakota. The rear panel of the armored skirt is in the raised position, for inspecting or servicing the idler and track. (3 ACR Museum)

Opposite below: This M2A2 Bradley fighting vehicle from an unidentified unit was photographed during the 1st Gulf War in 1991. The A2 versions were marked by flat armor plates bolted to the sides of the hull and the glacis (the trim vane was eliminated for this purpose); appliqué armor was attached to the turret; spaced, laminated armor on the hull rear; and new, flat armor plates replacing the original skirts. New headlight arrays and brush guards were introduced. (3 ACR Museum)

Above: 'THIS TOW'S FOR YOU' and a cartoon of Saddam Hussein are a bit of GI art found on a TOW launcher on a Bradley fighting vehicle during the 1st Gulf War. (3 ACR Museum)

Opposite above: During Operation Desert Storm in 1991, Major Constantine G. (Gus) Chamales, 2nd Squadron, 3rd Armored Cavalry Regiment, was photographed in his M3A2 Bradley somewhere in Iraq. Two flags, one American and the other unidentified, are waving over the vehicle. (3 ACR Museum)

Opposite below: Two Bradley M2 fighting vehicles have stopped next to a destroyed Iraqi T-72 main battle tank during Operation Desert Storm. The Bradley to the right has the sloped bustle storage rack characteristic of the M2 and M2A1. (DoD)

After the cease-fire at the conclusion of Operation Desert Storm, two M1A1 Abrams main battle tanks to the right and a lone M2A2 Bradley infantry fighting vehicle at the center are providing security for the 2nd Marine Division's area of responsibility, near Al Jahra, Kuwait. A knocked-out Iraqi T-72 tank is to the rear of the M2A2 Bradley. Orange air-recognition panels are on the turrets of all three US armored vehicles. (DoD)

Above: Railroad flatcars are delivering an M2 Bradley infantry fighting vehicle (foreground), an M109A2 155mm self-propelled howitzer, HEMTT Tanker, M1A1 Abrams main battle tanks, Multiple Launch Rocket Systems (MLRS), and other vehicles to be displayed in the National Victory Celebration in Washington DC in June 1991.This was a parade and observances in honor of the victory over Iraq during Operation Desert Storm. (DoD)

Opposite above: In another view of the same scene from a different angle, crewmen of the two Bradleys take a break next to an Iraqi T-72 knocked out by Coalition forces. On the TOW launcher on the Bradley to the right is the V sign of the 24th Infantry Division (Mechanized). (DoD)

Above: Both the M2A2 and the M3A2 Bradleys had the capability of mounting Explosive Reactive Armor (ERA) on their hulls and turrets. ERA countered the penetrating capabilities of shaped-charge shells and kinetic-energy penetrators by exploding on impact. This A2 Bradley fighting vehicle, photographed in Mogadishu in February 1994 while participating in United Nations Operation in Somalia II (UNOSOM II), is equipped with ERA. In the 1990s the US Army progressively updated its inventories of M2A2s and M3A2s, installing improvements based on lessons learned in Operation Desert Storm. Those improvements were designated ODS, an acronym for that operation. Some of the improvements in the M2A2 ODS and M3A2 ODS included: combat identification panels (CIP); thermal imaging for the driver; eye-safe laser rangefinder (ELRF); a GPS receiver and compass; and the Force XXI Battle Command Brigade and Below (FBCB2) Battlefield Command Information System. (DoD)

Opposite above: An M2A2 Bradley with ERA provides security for a US troop redeployment at the Port of Mogadishu during UNOSOM II in April 1994. A clear view is possible of the ERA tiles attached to the front of the vehicle. Markings on the final-drive assemblies are for Company B, 3rd Battalion, 15th Infantry Regiment, 24th Infantry Division (Mechanized). Note the headlight displays and their brush guards, reconfigured since the early M2/M3 Bradleys. (DoD)

Opposite below: A Bradley fighting vehicle assigned to the 412th Infantry Battalion, based in Baumholder, West Germany, is being loaded in a C-17 Globemaster III of the 17th Airlift Squadron, Charleston Air Force Base, South Carolina, in January 1996. The Bradley bears 'IFOR' markings for Implementation Force, a NATO peacekeeping force in Bosnia and Herzegovina during Operation Joint Endeavor. (DoD)

UN
UN

51 IFOR

Above: Two potential opposing military vehicles from before the fall of the Soviet Union, an A2 Bradley fighting vehicle (left) assigned to B troop, 3rd Squadron, 4th Cavalry Regiment, 2nd Brigade, 1st Armored Division, and a Russian Military Police BTR-80 Personnel Carrier and are parked side-by-side during friendlier times while on a joint patrol in support of Operation Joint Endeavor near Zvornic, Serbia, on February 29, 1996. Two Russian soldiers are standing on the glacis of the Bradley. (DoD)

Opposite above: On a dreary day in January 1996, an A2 Bradley fighting vehicle of 2nd Platoon, Company A, 4th Battalion, 12th Infantry, 2nd Brigade, 1st Armored Division, departs from Lodging Area Demi, battalion headquarters. Troops of this unit would be providing security for the engineers while exploding bunkers in the Zone of Separation between Bosnia and Herzegovina during Operation Joint Endeavor. (DoD)

Opposite below: An M2A2 Bradley infantry fighting vehicle of Bravo Company, 3rd Battalion, 5th Cavalry, serving with 1st Brigade, 1st Armor Division, Task Force Eagle, stands security in front of Check Point Alfa Two, on Route Arizona, located in Bosnia and Herzegovina, in support of Operation Joint Endeavor in February 1996. A spare bogie wheel is secured to the right side of the turret. (DoD)

Above: During Operation Joint Endeavor, near Camp Lisa in Bosnia in April 1996, members of Battery A, 94th Field Artillery Regiment, participating in Implementation Force (IFOR) are giving a demonstration of the M270 MLRS to Russian troops. Both vehicles are marked 'IFOR' on the launchers, and they are painted in NATO woodland camouflage. (DoD)

Opposite above: A US Army M2A2 Bradley infantry fighting vehicle marked with IFOR markings stands by at Task Force 1-26 Checkpoint W-30 outside Camp Demi in Bosnia, part of the American forces in Bosnia in support of Operation Joint Guard, an IFOR joint peacekeeping mission. Note the three horizontal strips of orange reflector tape near the rear of the hull, and the 'IFOR' and number 22 markings on the hull. 'LT. POWERS' is stenciled on the white stripe near the top of the side of the turret. (DoD)

Opposite below: Lieutenant Colonel Robin Swan, commander of TF 1-26 (Task Force 1st Battalion, 26th Infantry), standing third from left, along with several other officers, is being interviewed by a local reporter in front of a US Army M2A2 Bradley at a town in Bosnia and Herzegovina in February 1997. The Bradley is marked SFOR, for Stabilization Force, a NATO-led multinational peacekeeping force in Bosnia and Herzegovina following the Bosnian War. The number 23 is marked on the side of the hull. (DoD)

IFOR

SFOR
23

The burned-out remnants of an M2A2 Bradley infantry fighting vehicle that served with Bravo Company, 2nd Battalion, 2nd Infantry Regiment, 1st Infantry Division (Mechanized), are on a road in Bosnia and Herzegovina on May 26, 1997. A fire of unknown cause broke out in the M2A2 while returning from a force-protection mission. The occupants were able to toss out all ammunition, including five TOW missiles, and then were able to escape before the vehicle burst into flames. The roof and the sides of the hull collapsed, and the vehicle was a total loss. (DoD)

In 2003, 12 years after Operation Desert Storm, Bradley fighting vehicles once again saw combat against the Iraqis, with Operation Iraqi Freedom: the invasion of Iraq, which commenced on March 20 of that year. In this photo dated 23 March 2003, the crew of an M2A2 Bradley infantry fighting vehicle from the 24th Infantry Division, based at Fort Riley, Kansas, enjoys a brief break during the advance through Central Iraq. Visible to the sides of the 25mm gun are two storage boxes for smoke grenades. (DoD)

Opposite below: Vehicle commander Sergeant Mike Stacher, Bravo Battery, 6th Battalion, 37th Field Artillery, gives verbal directions to the driver of his mud-spattered M270A1 Multiple Launch Rocket System (MLRS) during a combined training exercise with the Republic of Korea's 3rd ROK Corps at Kwo Suck Jong training area during October 1998. Armored shutters were provided for the cab windshields; two of the shutters are swung downward, while the left shutter is in the raised position. (DoD)

Above: On 3 April 2003, Coalition forces led by the US 3rd Infantry Division began battling their way into Baghdad. In this photo dated 16 April, while the city was still being secured, a Bradley infantry fighting vehicle from the 3rd Infantry Division stands watch near the presidential palace of Saddam Hussein. The panels that have the appearance of louvers or Venetian blinds, located on the two rear storage boxes and at the center of the hull, are combat identification panels (CIDs). These panels, when viewed through infrared sights, had a distinctive appearance, which alerted Coalition gunners to the fact that the vehicle was a friendly one. (DoD)

Opposite above: A crewman relaxes in the scant shade at the bow of an M6 Bradley Linebacker at the security checkpoint at 3rd Infantry Division D-Main entrance at Stop Point Chippewa in central Iraq on 2 April 2003. The M6 Bradley Linebacker was an air-defense version of the vehicle, based on the M2A2 ODS, with the TOW missile launcher replaced by a four-tube Stinger anti-aircraft missile launcher. (DoD)

Opposite below: Doing duty as an improvised bulldozer, an M2A2 ODS Bradley infantry fighting vehicle from Alpha Company, 3rd Battalion, 15th Infantry Regiment is toppling a mural of former Iraqi President Saddam Hussein at the Yarmuk Hospital in Baghdad during Operation Iraqi Freedom. A large bin fabricated from welded metal slats has been mounted on the side of the vehicle for stowing crew duffel bags. (DoD)

/32

41

Above: At Baghdad International Airport (formerly Saddam International Airport) on 8 April 2003, an A2 ODS Bradley fighting vehicle is standing guard over two Black Hawk helicopters assigned to the V Corps Command Post. The crew of the Bradley has placed a box under the ramp, to provide them with a horizontal working platform. (DoD)

Below: An A2 ODS Bradley fighting vehicle provides perimeter security outside the terminal at Baghdad International Airport on 8 April 2003. A few days earlier, after fierce battle, US forces had taken control of this airport, which would be a crucial logistical base for Coalition forces in the years ahead. (DoD)

Above: US soldiers pause around a Bradley fighting vehicle to examine a dead civilian in a ditch in August 2003 during Operation Iraqi Freedom. From the smiles on the faces of the GIs, the deceased presumably was an insurgent. The final-drive assemblies of the Bradley have markings for E Troop, 2nd Squadron, 3rd Armored Cavalry Regiment. (DoD)

Below: During Operation Iraqi Freedom, US soldiers, possibly a munitions disposal team, are examining two discarded Iraqi S-125/SA-3 anti-aircraft missiles at an unidentified location. To the left is a Bradley fighting vehicle, and to the right is an M113A3. (DoD)

Above: Members of 1st Squadron, 3rd Armored Cavalry Regiment, return to base after supporting dismounted troops during Operation Rifle Sweep, on 26 November 2003. This was a cordon-and-search operation for weapons and munitions held by insurgents and anti-Coalition forces along the Iraq-Syria border. A spare sprocket is stored on the bow of the Bradley. (DoD)

Opposite above: The commander of an M2A2 Bradley infantry fighting vehicle watches from his hatch as a monument to Saddam Hussein is being toppled in Al Hawijah during the Operation Bayonet Lightning phase of Operation Iraqi Freedom in 2003. The mud-spattered black panel to the rear of the triangular front armor panel on the hull was a recognition device, easily visible through infrared sights. (DoD)

Opposite below: In a photo related to the preceding one, an M2A2 Bradley is bulldozing part of a monument to Saddam in Al Hawijah, Iraq. On top of the Integrated Sight Unit is a box-shaped object: this is a mounting bracket for an anti-tank missile countermeasures device, which was to have been part of the ODS improvements but was not used operationally. (DoD)

Above: A Bradley fighting vehicle knocked out in the Iraqi desert exhibits heavy damage on its left rear quarter, with armored skirting missing and what appears to be an opening from a projectile penetration on the hull sponson above the visible section of track. The black recognition panel towards the front of the hull has flopped down, loose from its rear fastenings. (3 ACR Museum)

Opposite above: A Bradley fighting vehicle from Task Force 1st Battalion, 150th Armor Regiment, West Virginia Army National Guard, has just fired a TOW missile during a Joint Air and Artillery training exercise at Camp Caldwell, Diyala Province, Iraq, on 14 October 2004. The blast from the launching has stirred up dust on the rear deck of the Bradley. (DoD)

Opposite below: An M2A3 Bradley infantry fighting vehicle of 1st Platoon, Apache Troop, 2nd Battalion, 5th Cavalry, patrols for insurgents during a combat operation in Fallujah, Iraq, on 9 November 2004. The explosive reactive armor (ERA) on the Bradley fighting vehicles was designed to defeat the RPG-7 anti-tank rounds with which enemy forces were plentifully supplied. (DoD)

Above: Bradley fighting vehicles, part of a column transporting troops from 1st Battalion, 128th Infantry, Wisconsin National Guard, and 2nd Battalion, 108th Infantry, New York National Guard, prepare to move out on a patrol to Ad Dujayl, Iraq, on 21 December 2004. The Bradley in the foreground is painted in NATO woodland camouflage, with sand-colored ERA tiles, while the Bradley in the rear is painted overall in sand-colored paint. (DoD)

Opposite above: Troopers from the 2nd Squadron, 11th Armored Cavalry Regiment, prepare to advance alongside an M2A2 Bradley into a bunker area during a raid on the Hateen Weapons Complex in Babil, Iraq, on 26 March 2005. Painted in black on the TOW missile launcher is a skull and crossbones, and 'Say Hello to My Little Friend', a familiar line from the movie *Scarface*. (DoD)

Opposite below: Civilians look on during April 2005 as this A2 Bradley fighting vehicle of the 1st Battalion, 30th Infantry (Wild Boar) 3rd Brigade, 3rd Infantry Division, Task Force Liberty, provides security to infantry conducting a search for weapons and insurgents near Ba'qûbah, Diyâlá Province, Iraq, during Operation Iraqi Freedom. This Bradley is equipped with a suite of ERA modules, capable of defeating, among other threats, the rocket-propelled grenades popular with insurgents. A few of these modules are missing, including one in the first position on the near side of the vehicle hull. Visible are the two vertical brackets used to mount the ERA module. Also missing is the forward side skirt panel. Stowed on the glacis is a roll of concertina wire, which would be used in setting up a perimeter defense for the vehicle. (Department of Defense)

An M88A1 Recovery Vehicle from A Troop, 5-7 Cavalry, 1st Brigade, 3rd Infantry Division (Mechanized), is using its boom to remove the power pack from a Bradley fighting vehicle at Logistical Support Area Anaconda, Balad, Iraq, in May 2005. In the foreground is the engine compartment of the Bradley. The power pack is a unit that can be pulled all at once from the vehicle within about 30 minutes. Its main components are the Cummins VTA-903T engine, the radiator assembly (over the engine), and the General Electric HMPT-500-3 or -3EC transmission. (3 ACR Museum)

Bradley fighting vehicles, especially those with additional armor, provided protection to their occupants from a number of munitions, but not all of them. This image and the following two depict Bradleys that were destroyed and were taken to depots to await final disposition. This view is from the left side, showing the A2 hull and skirt armor. (3 ACR Museum)

Opposite below: Scouts from Task Force 1-15 (1st Battalion, 15th Infantry Regiment) are laboriously making their way through deep sand during a mission in June 2005. The Bradley fighting vehicle, which seems to be maneuvering to recover the mired HMMWV, is equipped with ERA tiles on the hull and the turret. Another Bradley, turret turned to the rear, is in the right background. (3 ACR Museum)

Above: The destroyed Bradley is seen from the rear. The explosion that destroyed the vehicle collapsed the roof; part of the turret has fallen into the interior of the hull; some of its frontal armor, the 25mm gun and mantlet, and the ISU are in view. (3 ACR Museum)

Opposite above: This is another destroyed Bradley fighting vehicle, with little recognizable save for tracks, torn-apart hull armor, and part of the vertical appliqué armor. (3 ACR Museum)

Opposite below: A mine caused heavy damage to this M6 Bradley Linebacker. Most of the suspension on the left side was destroyed, and many appliqué armor and skirt panels were blown off. Two Bradleys are standing by in the background. This vehicle, though unfit for further combat, was cosmetically restored and is in the collection of the US Army Air Defense Artillery Museum, Fort Sill, Ok. (3 ACR Museum)

Above: Sergeant Lucas Wolfe, the gunner of a Bradley Linebacker with 5th Battalion, 7th Cavalry, Task Force Liberty, studies the horizon for threats while manning an observation post in Balad, Iraq, in September 2005. The 5th Battalion often conducted surveillance in this area, which overlooked a road frequently used by insurgents who planted improvised explosive devices (IEDs) along the route in hopes of inflicting damage on Coalition troops and vehicles. (3 ACR Museum)

Opposite above: A rocket has just been fired by an MLRS from B Company, 3rd Battalion, 13th Field Artillery, 42nd Division Artillery, outside Tikrit, Iraq, during Operation Iraqi Freedom, in June 2005. The launching of even one missile from an MLRS could kick up a significant amount of dust in the Iraqi desert. (DoD)

Opposite below: An armored recovery vehicle (the boom is visible) is moving the remains of a destroyed Bradley fighting vehicle. Part of the supplemental armor has been torn off, and substantial damage has been inflicted on the rear of the hull, which is missing at least part of its floor. (3 ACR Museum)

As part of efforts to improve crew protection on Bradley fighting vehicles from threats from insurgents and IEDs, the Army began installing a transparent armor gun shield (TAGS) to partially surround the commander's hatch. That feature, which had ballistic-glass panels in a rigid frame, is present on this M2A2 ODS Bradley infantry fighting vehicle from the 1st Battalion, 3rd Armored Combat Regiment, seen conducting cordon-and-search operations in the city of Biaj, Iraq, in January 2006. (DoD)

Mechanics from Troop B, 1st Squadron, 7th Cavalry Regiment, maneuver a power pack into one of their unit's M2A3 Bradley infantry fighting vehicles at Camp Taji, Iraq, on 1 December 2006. A sling attached to the engine is being lifted by a crane, which is out of view. The man on the ground is steadying the transmission. Note the damage to the supplemental hull armor to the right. (3 ACR Museum)

Above: After detonating an IED at a site in Iraq, members of Explosive Ordnance Disposal Group I are returning to Forward Operating Base Taji on 19 February 2007. The Bradley, the turret of which is traversed to the rear, is provided with ERA (note the rough texture on the center area of each ERA tile) and a transparent armor gun shield for the commander. Following in the background is a mine resistant ambush protected (MRAP) vehicle. (DoD)

Opposite above: A Bradley fighting vehicle accompanies troopers from D Company, 2nd Battalion, 12th Cavalry Regiment, 2nd Brigade Combat Team, 1st Cavalry Division, during a cordon-and-search mission in Ghazaliya, Iraq, on 9 February 2007. A camouflage net nicknamed the dome tent has been rigged on a frame over the turret roof, to make it harder for enemy snipers to pick off the gunner and the commander when they are standing in their hatches. A spare sprocket is stored on the bow. (DoD)

Opposite below: The crew of a Bradley fighting vehicle of the 1st Battalion, 8th Cavalry Regiment, are setting off for a patrol from Camp Rustamiyah to the Baladiat area of Baghdad, Iraq, on 15 February 2007. This is an A3 version of the Bradley, as indicated by the CITV on the right rear of the turret. (DoD)

Above: Soldiers of Task Force 2-7 CAV, 2nd Battalion, 7th Cavalry Regiment provide security with their M2A2 Bradley fighting vehicle in front of a restaurant in Hit, Iraq, on 29 April 2007. Without ERA tiles installed on the vehicle, a good view is available of the supplemental armor on the hull and the turret. On the hull side armor are clips for attaching ERA. (DoD)

Opposite above: Partially obscured in a shroud of gun smoke from the 25mm cannon, a Bradley fighting vehicle of Company B, 2nd Battalion, 136th Combined Arms Battalion, 1/34 Brigade Combat Team, engages two fleeing vehicles during an operation southwest of Camp Fallujah, Iraq, on 9 February 2007. The Bradley fired ten rounds at the two vehicles. (DoD)

Opposite below: US Army Private First Class Mark Purcell, a member of the 1st Battalion, 15th Infantry Regiment, 3rd Brigade, 3rd Infantry Division, is about to load his gear into an A2 Bradley fighting vehicle for Operation Chalons, a cordon-and-search security mission in Jisr Diyala, Iraq, 23 April 2007. Two large rolls of razor wire are strapped to the side of the hull. In the background is an Abrams main battle tank. (DoD)

A US Army Bradley A2 fighting vehicle crewed by members of the 4th Battalion, 64th Armored Regiment, 4th Brigade Combat Team, 3rd Infantry Division, is at Forward Operating Base Falcon, prepared to embark on clearing operations in the Rashid district of Baghdad on 1 January 2008. Over the turret is camouflage netting supported by metal bows, to offer some shade, to camouflage the commander and the gunner when standing in their hatches, and to repel grenades. (DoD)

A US Army Bradley fighting vehicle, equipped with ERA and a ballistic shield for the commander's station on the turret, patrols a market during a clearing operation in Kesra, Iraq, on 24 February 2008. Note how the headlight assemblies and their brush guards have been remounted on top of the lower outboard ERA tiles. (DoD)

Opposite below: A large sign in Arabic and English on the back of a Bradley M3A3 cavalry fighting vehicle from Troop G, 2nd Squadron, 3rd Armored Cavalry, warns following vehicles to remain 100 meters behind the Bradley. At the time, in August 2010, the vehicle was engaged in Operation Raider Harvest in Diyala Province, Iraq. With the Bradley's turret turned to the right, the CITV is prominently displayed next to the commander's transparent armor gun shield. (DoD)

Above: A US Army Bradley fighting vehicle leads a patrol through a marketplace in Kesra Village, Iraq, on 24 February 2008. The marketplace was notorious for the presence of Al-Qaeda fighters in it, and the locals called it the Al-Qaeda Capitol. Towards the rear of the hull is a recently introduced innovation in the struggle to defeat the plague of improvised explosive devices (IEDs) that were so destructive against Coalition forces: an antenna for a jamming system intended to neutralize radio-controlled IEDs. Note also the spotlight in a flexible, yoke-type holder on top of each headlight brush guard: a close examination reveals that each holder is secured by a large wing nut on the underside of the top of the brush guard. (DoD)

Opposite above: An A2 Bradley fighting vehicle provides security for soldiers from Alpha Company, 1st Battalion, 15th Infantry Regiment, 3rd Heavy Brigade Combat Team, 3rd Infantry Division, who are performing a clearing operation with local Abna'a al-Iraq (Sons of Iraq) through a series of villages south of Salman Pak, Iraq, on 16 February 2008. A number of ERA tiles are missing from the glacis, permitting a view of the mounting brackets for the tiles. (DoD)

Opposite below: A Bradley fighting vehicle with a dome tent for the commander and gunner and an antenna for an anti-IED radio jammer is providing security for members of Company D, 1st Battalion, 8th Infantry Regiment, on a patrol of Mosul, Iraq, on 1 April 2010. In the foreground is Private First Class Adam Devries. (DoD)

Above: Looking on and communicating by hand-held radio as a Bradley fighting vehicle approaches with its turret pointing to the rear is 1st Lieutenant Donald Maloy, leader of 1st Platoon, Company D, 1st Battalion, 8th Infantry Regiment. The Bradley was providing cordon security during a joint Iraqi Army and Coalition forces clearing operation in the al-Sinaa neighborhood of Mosul, 1 April 2010. Of particular interest are the array of four spotlights on the ERA tiles on the glacis, the dome tent over the turret roof, and the anti-IED antenna towards the left rear of the hull roof. In addition to protecting the crew of the turret, the dome tent had an insulated, bow-type frame that protected the crew and the antennas from the low-hanging power lines sometimes encountered in street fighting in Iraq. (DoD)

Opposite above: Members of Troop E of an unidentified cavalry unit are unloading equipment from their A3 Bradley fighting vehicle at Camp Beuhring, Kuwait, on 10 September 2011, in preparation for their role in Operation New Dawn, as Operation Iraqi Freedom was renamed as of 1 September 2010. These men have removed the barrel of the 25mm gun from its receiver. An eagle is painted on the panel on the right front of the turret; this panel, which had a piano hinge in the center, was part of the vehicle's combat identification system. On the armored doors of the Integrated Sight Unit are black stencils warning against pushing or pulling the doors, but to use the internal handle only. (DoD)

Opposite below: Turret traversed to the right, an M2A3 Bradley from the 1st Battalion, 68th Armor Regiment, part of the 3rd Advise and Assist Brigade, 4th Infantry Division, churns up dust as it proceeds to a training session at the gunnery range at Camp Buehring, Kuwait, 20 October 2011. The ERA tiles are not mounted on the hull and the glacis of this vehicle, permitting a rare view of the mounting brackets for those tiles. This vehicle may be distinguished as an M2A3, not an M3A3, by the presence of periscopes to the rear of the cargo hatch. (DoD)

Above: The warhead of a BGM-71 TOW missile is just emerging from the front of the launcher on a Bradley from the 1st Armored Brigade Combat Team, 1st Infantry Division, during a live-fire exercise at the Udairi Range Complex, Kuwait, on 22 January 2011. (DoD)

Opposite above: In a companion view to the preceding one, two M2A3 Bradleys of the 1st Armored Brigade Combat Team, 1st Infantry Division, are engaged in a live-fire exercise at the Udairi Range on 22 January 2011. The vehicle to the right has just fired a BGM-71 missile, whose folding fins are just starting to deploy. (DoD)

Opposite below: An M2A2 Bradley from the 1st Armor Brigade Combat Team, 3rd Infantry Division, proceeds along a dirt road at a firing range at Fort Stewart, Georgia, while conducting Table XII gunnery on 7 December 2016. Names of three members of the vehicle crew are stenciled in black on the TOW launcher, on the rear of which is a shiny, olive drab colored dust cover. (DoD)

Above: Making tracks at a firing range at Fort Stewart, Georgia, on 7 December 2016, is an M2A2 Bradley, possibly the same one shown in the preceding photograph. Note the black identification panel on the side of the forward part of the hull. (DoD)

Opposite above: An M2A3 Bradley from the 1st Battalion, 64th Armor Regiment, advances on a gravel road during a company combined-arms live-fire exercise at Fort Stewart, Georgia, on 7 February 2017. The glacis and the hull are camouflaged with pine bows and netting. As is often seen on Bradleys, a spare sprocket is stored on the lower front end of the vehicle. (DoD)

Opposite below: A crane truck is hoisting an A3 Bradley fighting vehicle onto a flatbed truck, from which it will be transferred to the USNS *Mendonca* (T-AKR-303), a roll-on, roll-off vehicle-cargo ship, at Shuaiba Port, Kuwait, on 28 February 2017. This may be an M3A3 Bradley cavalry fighting vehicle, as there are indistinct Cavalry markings on the right final-drive assembly. (DoD)

Above: M2A3 Bradley infantry fighting vehicles assigned to Company B, 1st Battalion, 8th Infantry Regiment, 3rd Armored Brigade Combat Team, 4th Infantry Division, are about to depart for a live-fire exercise at the Karliki Range, Zagan, Poland, on 2 February 2017. This brigade was conducting realistic live-fire training to prepare for exercises across Europe, as part of Atlantic Resolve: an operation to enhance deterrence capabilities in the region, improve the US's ability to respond to potential crises, and defend allies and partners in Europe. (DoD)

Opposite above: The crew of this M2A3 Bradley are all smiles while departing from the qualification area at a live-fire training exercise at the Karliki Range, Zagan, Poland, on 2 February 2017. They are assigned to Company B, 1st Battalion, 8th Infantry Regiment, 3rd Armored Brigade Combat Team, 4th Infantry Division. Clips for mounting ERA tiles are on the side of the supplemental hull armor. (DoD)

Opposite below: Two M2A3 Bradley infantry fighting vehicles from Alpha Company, 8th Brigade Engineer Battalion, are returning to base after participating in a breaching exercise with the 9th Cavalry at the Rodriguez Live Fire Complex, Republic of Korea, on 10 August 2017. The vehicle commander has a shortened transparent armor gun shield. (DoD)

Three crewmen of an M3A3 Bradley cavalry fighting vehicle (note the periscopes on the cargo hatch: a feature of the M3 CFVs) of the 5th Squadron, 4th Cavalry Regiment, 2nd Armored Brigade Combat Team, 1st Infantry Division, are gathered around the rear of their vehicle, awaiting their turn to conduct a firing-systems check at the Presidenski Range, Trzebien, Poland, on 20 September 2017. This brigade was part-way through its ten-day preparation period to be mission-ready. Note the antennas mounted on the tops of the brush guards of the taillights. (DoD)

Appendix

BRADLEY GENERAL DATA

MODEL	M2A3	M3A3
WEIGHT^ (LB)	64000	64000
LENGTH (IN)	258	258
WIDTH (IN)	129	129
HEIGHT (IN)	117	117
TRACK (IN)	96	96
STD TRACK WIDTH (IN)	21	21
MAX SPEED (MPH)	38	38
FUEL CAPACITY (US GALLONS)	175	175
RANGE (MILES)	250	250
ELECTRICAL	24 volt negative ground	24 volt negative ground
TURNING RADIUS (FT)	PIVOT	PIVOT

^Fighting weight without armor tiles, tiles add 8,000 pounds.

ENGINE DATA

ENGINE MAKE/MODEL	Cummins VTA-903T
NUMBER OF CYLINDERS	V-8
CUBIC INCH DISPLACEMENT	903
HORSEPOWER	600 @ 2600 RPM
TORQUE (LB-FT)	1025 @ 2350 RPM